I CAN!

THE KEY TO LIFE'S GOLDEN SECRETS

by

BEN SWEETLAND

Radio's Consulting Psychologist

Melvin Powers
Wilshire Book Company

12015 Sherman Road, No. Hollywood, CA 91605

DEDICATED TO THE ONE WHO, IN
MY LIFE, IS MY LITTLE GIRL, MY
SWEETHEART—AND WIFE; EDEL.

CONTENTS

7

"I Can!"

These four letters—in an unusual way—lifted a dejected, despondent man from the depths of despair to the heights of success and happiness.

In New York City I once gave a series of weekly lectures under the general title of: "The Road to Happiness." A man, in his late fifties, attended regularly, hoping that through the messages I was giving, he would find the magic thought which would elevate him to a place where he could support his wife, instead of being supported by her.

The job he had held for years came to an end and in trying to find another one, he was constantly confronted with the statement: "You're too old."

Week after week Bill Jones (we'll call him) arrived for the lecture, with an expectant look on his face, but would leave with the feeling that his pursuit of an answer to his problem had been fruitless.

There was an exception to this weekly routine—something happened. Ending a lecture and approaching Bill—instead of seeing his long drawn face—there was an expression of great exuberance. "I've got the answer!" he exclaimed with a tone of actual excitement. Naturally I was happy—and eager to learn just what it was that turned the tide from depression to ecstasy.

Bill took me to the chair where he had been sitting and pointed to a visible portion of an electric sign which was mounted on the top of a building several blocks away. The word "American" was part of the wording of the sign —and where Bill sat—he could see but the last four letters, ICAN.

"There's the answer to my problem, Ben," he said with excitement. "Up to now I have been thinking in terms of 'I Can't,'" and continuing said, "all evening those four letters have been glaring at me—as though intended as a message from above especially for me.

"I CAN, Ben," Bill declared, "and tomorrow I am going to prove it."

Bill did prove it. He landed a job as a simple laborer in a flour mill and started to climb until he reached the position of general manager, and with a very satisfactory income.

The heights to which you climb in this life depends wholly on how completely you have accepted the four letters comprising the title of this book: "I Can!"

Reading the book once—*thoughtfully*—will open new vistas of opportunity and happiness for you. Reading it a second time will add further stimulus to your new resolutions. And—perusing the pages a third time, will fire you with an unbounded ambition which will glow in intensity until you attain your most cherished objectives.

I have not attempted a literary masterpiece—just a frank *me* to *you* revelation of the principles I have discovered to be so effective.

Humbly, your author,
Ben Sweetland

SECTION ONE

In Which the Dynamic, Power-Building, Happiness-Giving Secrets Are Revealed

CHAPTER ONE

Getting Acquainted With Yourself

You ARE NOW starting on the greatest adventure of your life—*IF*—yes, *if* you will read this first chapter with a mind freed from previously formed opinions, skepticism, prejudices—and *think* while you read.

At this point I will not ask you to agree with me, any more than I would want you to disagree with what I am about to say.

The late John Wanamaker, the Merchant Prince as he was called by his contemporaries, seldom refused an audience to a salesman. He claimed that by listening to them he learned of new items coming on the market, but he prided himself in the thought: "I defy any man to sell me a thing I do not want." It is with this Wanamaker attitude I ask you to approach the thoughts you will find contained in this book. The enthusiasm which will result; the inspiration you will gain; the happiness you will find— and the success you will achieve will be of your own making—because your acceptance of the principles will come from your own reasoning, not that they were forced upon you

Russell Conwell, in his world famous book, "Acres of Diamonds," through countless illustrations, showed that human beings were constantly searching elsewhere for the very things they had at hand. Although he didn't say so, he could easily have meant the power which brings leadership; self-mastery; health and happiness.

Our outstanding leaders occupy their positions because of the power they have within. The heights to which you will climb will be the result of your use of the power you now possess.

You have lived with yourself all of your life, yet—unless you now have everything you want in life—you do not know yourself.

Ninety-five percent of all motorists are driving cars without anything but a vague understanding of that which is under the hood. They know that by feeding oil and gasoline to the car, and by manipulating buttons, pedals and steering wheel, the automobile will provide transportation. However, the driver with an understanding of the vehicle's complex mechanism, can operate with far greater efficiency. He will obtain more miles per gallon of gasoline; his tires will give increased mileage. And, his car will be giving good performance when other cars of the same age are being discarded as worthless.

Most of us are merely existing because we do nothing more than the obvious things; eat, drink and sleep. When we learn something about the human mechanism—and particularly the mind which controls it—there are no limits to the heights we can climb.

On one occasion I had an opportunity of visiting one of the country's finest laboratories. Room after room were filled with chemicals of every known description. Other rooms were replete with scientific instruments. I marvelled as the chemist explained the purposes for which the multiplicity of devices were intended. After the tour was completed, and I had about exhausted my vocabulary of adjectives and superlatives, the scientist concluded by saying: "With everything we have, and which represents the efforts of the world's greatest scientists, this laboratory, as great as it appears to be, does not compare with the laboratory each and every one has in his own physical being." "Right now," he continued, "the laboratory in your body is busily engaged digesting the food you ate at lunch, extracting from it the elements necessary for blood, bone, tissue and energy. No laboratory in existence is equipped with the instruments or skill, to perform such a task."

In the field of photography, there is a new development in the form of a camera which will deliver finished prints in just a minute after the picture has been snapped. "Wonderful," you exclaim—but think of the human camera *we* have. We glance at an object and instantaneously the image is carried to the brain.

We marvel at sound recording. Through the use of electronics sound can be recorded on discs, wire or tape This result, as interesting—and valuable—as it is, does not begin to compare with our own human recording system. The ear—our microphone—receives the vibratory impressions which are at once recorded in the gray matter of the brain, and which can later be repeated through the voice.

Right now you might be growing a bit suspicious. You

may say to yourself: "Yes, perhaps I can gain a bit if I become a physiologist," and, you think, "it would take me years to learn all of that." Of course, this is not correct. We are constantly living through a series of habits. Success, happiness and well-being comes, not from added burdens, but by merely substituting right habits for wrong ones. The object of this opening chapter is to give you a slight idea of wonderful, amazing you.

Have you ever watched men and machinery excavating for a new structure? Perhaps you, as I, have marvelled at the humanlike operation of the giant steam shovel. You would see the boom lowered, the huge shovel digging into the earth and picking up hundreds of pounds of material; then easily swing around and dump it into a waiting truck. Should you go into the cabin and watch the operator, you would see him surrounded by a myriad of levers. One lowers the boom, another presses it forward and raises it; another swings it around, and still another operates the jaws of the scoop of shovel, permitting the earth or rock to drop into any receptacle which might be beneath it. Yes, it is astonishing—and seems almost alive. But what do we have within our human bodies? Think of the intricate network of cords and muscles brought into play each time we stoop over to pick up an object!

One time a man who thought he was about the poorest of the poor told me he did not have a single thing of financial value. That same morning I had read in a Philadelphia paper an article to the effect that a man who had lost the sight in one of his eyes had offered the sum of $10,000 to anyone who would sell him an eye which could be transplanted. I asked this chap if he would sell one of his own. He indignantly told me he wouldn't, yet, just a few moments previously he had told me he had absolutely nothing on which he could raise a dime.

So far I have given you just a few illustrations regarding the physical portion of our being and how man has been unable to duplicate the functions of any part of the body notwithstanding unlimited financial resources which might be drawn upon in such an endeavor.

For a moment, consider the mental aspects of being. Man has been able to create instruments which would do certain things usually done by mind. We have machines which can add, subtract, multiply and divide; we have much automatic equipment which performs many operations mechanically. All of these, however, are the product of mind. And, for each type of operation a specific machine or instrument is required. The human mind is capable of performing all of them.

By now, if you have been *thinking* while reading, you are beginning to sense that you do possess a body so amazing that a vast amount of study and research would be required in fully comprehending all that it does encompass. "So what?" you may proclaim. "Suppose I have a wonderful body," you think, "what has it done for me?" If such a question has come into your mind, it is a good indication, and, as you continue to read you will learn that you, as you are now, have all that is needed to enable you to acquire riches, better health, and, above all, happiness.

If you are a normal individual you have, at times, envied others for possessions they have and which you would like to have. They may have a better job, a business of their own, a fine home, a fabulous bank account. All right!

Let us see if we can find the difference between the one who is highly successful and the one who is not.

Is the difference physical? You immediately agree it is not because the failure might even be better off physically, than the one who has acquired riches.

Is the difference educational? At first you might feel inclined to think it is, but as you ponder you recall the names of many who have fine educations and who are failures, while on the other side you know of those with but little education who have gone places.

And, while making comparisons, ask yourself what the real difference is—why is one a success, the other a failure? What does the success possess which is lacking in the failure? Each has the same type of marvelous body as we previously discussed, and, if both of them are normal, each has the same kind of mind. The real difference is one of Life's Golden Secrets, which will be revealed as you continue to read.

Some years ago, I recall visiting a large men's furnishing establishment with a friend of mine. He went in to do a bit of shopping, he said. My envy was certainly aroused to watch this man as he went from counter to counter. He stopped at the sport shirts department. Without once asking the price, he would look around and point to various shirts, saying: "I'll take that one, and this one, and you might include three of those, etc." When he reached sweaters, he did the same, selecting three or four. At the necktie rack he picked them as nonchalantly as one would pick flowers in the garden, ending up with perhaps a hundred dollars' worth of ties. Several dozen pairs of socks were selected, as well as a large number of suits of underwear. All in all, he obligated himself for several hundred dollars in a matter of about 10 minutes, doing so as casually as one might drop into a cigar store for a pack of cigarettes. At that time my circumstances were such that I would have to think of my finances in order to buy as much as a single shirt. The contrast between me and this liberal spender was such that it seemed incredible that I would ever be able to do as much.

Have you ever watched a magician do a trick which baffled you completely? It seemed so mystifying that one would almost think the magician had some mystic help from the other side. Then, after the bit of magic had been exposed and explained, it appeared so simple, it seemed almost foolish.

I now can go on a spending spree like my friend, should I wish to do so, and as I look back to the time when circumstances prevented me from doing it, the means of transition were so simple, I almost feel apologetic for ever having been in a situation where I was forced to count pennies. A girl, in her early twenties, once came to me with a tale of woe. She had a good voice—and knew she could sing—but she was sure she could never do anything with her talent. As we talked about singers of note, the look of dismay in her face plainly showed her certainty that such prominence was never meant for her. I spent several minutes in introducing this young lady to herself, using practically the same words as you have read so far. Slowly a light dawned and she began to understand that, basically, there was little difference between her and those she had envied. This once discouraged miss has since appeared, triumphantly, on the concert stage in most of the large cities in this country.

Have you ever rejoiced over a sleepless night? Perhaps not! There was one man, however, who considers a sleepless night as the turning point in his life. Upon retiring, his troubles did tend toward keeping him awake. He had obligations about to fall due, and, at the time, he could not see his way clear in meeting them. A question he asked himself caused him to completely change his trend of thought into channels which lead to a glorious life of security and contentment. The question? "What is the matter with me that I cannot take care of my obligations with the ease that so many others do?" The rest of the night he spent making a mental analysis of himself. He reached the same conclusions as are being drawn in this first chapter—that all men are born equal. During the long, dark hours of the night he compared himself with those he knew who were in comfortable circumstances and found in every case that they possessed nothing he did not possess—except, perhaps, the consciousness: "I Can!"

Before the first rays of dawn started painting streaks of gold on the clouds, one of life's golden secrets began seeping into this man's consciousness. Instead of arising drowsy and weary as might be expected after a sleepless night, he alighted with the verve of a child on Christmas morning. What happened to this man? Within a year he was in a position where he had a big income, was having a new home designed and built, and had plans for taking his family on a thrilling European vacation.

Although the results which may be obtained through the use of this book will sound like fiction, the book itself is not to be read as one would read a book of fiction. You are to *think* as you read—and to properly do this, you should break up your reading time with sufficient pauses to allow for adequate mental digestion.

It would be possible to read this entire chapter in from twelve to twenty minutes. I would much prefer that you take at least an hour on these preliminary pages. Get yourself comfortable and fully relaxed. See to it that the lighting is sufficient to avoid eye strain. Then read the chapter paragraph by paragraph. Pause after each one and reflect; think about that which you read to make certain you fully comprehend the meaning intended. As you read the illustrations given, know that the blessings which came to those mentioned can also come to you.

There is one more instance I would like to relate before bringing this chapter to a close. A student who had been attending my course on Creative Psychology at a local college, in a plaintive tone of voice, asked me if he could talk to me for a few moments after class. I granted his request. After a brief hesitation he began: "Dr. Sweetland, I believe everything you say is true, and that it is possible for one to succeed in life if he follows the right principles, but I can't see it for myself." I asked why. At first it was an effort for him to get down to his basic trouble, then, as though forcing himself, he looked me in the eye and replied: "I'm not good enough. I've done lots of things in my life of which I am deeply ashamed, and I can't feel that I am entitled to have the good things of life. It would seem unfair for me to make great headway while others who have lived cleaner lives would have to struggle along for a bare existence."

I asked this young man if he would try to make amends for his mistakes should he become an outstanding success. "Oh, yes, certainly!" he promptly replied. Then I brought up another query: "Wouldn't the world be a better place in which to live, then, should you take advantage of that which you already possess and make a great success in life?" He had to admit that the answer was yes.

Perhaps loss of self-respect is one of the main reasons why people are held back in life. They inwardly feel they are not entitled to success and happiness. Were they to stop to reason, they would find that with the right attitude, by gaining success, they could make up for many of the wrongs they might have done.

*   *   *

In this book, one dominant or major thought will be advanced in each chapter, and you are earnestly urged to stay with each chapter until you have thoroughly absorbed its main thought.

Right now, before reading further, ask yourself: "What is the dominant thought in this chapter?" If you have been seriously weighing each statement made, the correct answer will come to you. "I CAN—I Can be a success!"

In a later chapter you will learn why I am making this suggestion, but, between now and the time you begin Chapter Two, I want you to burn those five words into your consciousness. Every time you think of it, say to yourself: "I CAN be a success." Make the statement several times upon arising in the morning; many times during the day, and, without fail, repeat it again and again before retiring. And, as you say the words, do so with a note of elation. Back the words with gladness—and emphasis.

When you, as a child, wanted to go somewhere very badly, but doubted that you could, can you recall your tone of voice when you found you could go? "I *can* go," you sang aloud. That is the emotion you are to put behind the words, "I CAN be a success."

I suggest you allow two to three days to elapse before beginning Chapter Two. In the meantime, with unbounded enthusiasm: "I CAN be a success!"

Your Pledge to Yourself!

"PUT THAT IN writing!" When two or more people enter into any kind of a business arrangement of importance, a contract is usually entered into. This is done to provide a proper record of the obligation of the partners and to offer a means of prompting the parties thereto to live up to their written promises.

How about the promises one makes to oneself? Suppose you were to call upon a lawyer and ask him to draw up a contract between you and yourself. He would gaze upon you with suspicion, and wonder when your keeper would be after you. As ludicrous as this statement appears, we would be better off were we to become obligated in some specific manner for the promises we make to ourselves.

If children did not obey their parents any better than human beings obey themselves, it would be a pathetic situation indeed. If you asked your child to do a certain thing the following day, you would expect him to do it, and if he didn't, you, most likely, would take him to task for having ignored your instruction. How many times do you tell yourself that on the following day you will do a certain thing—and then when the following day arrives, you do nothing about it? How many times have you promised yourself that you will overcome or modify certain habits—and then you fail to do so?

I might even refer to the annual New Year's resolutions. How many do you keep? With some people, I would be safe in asking, "Have you kept *any* of them?"

Some will impair their health through faulty living habits. They will promise themselves to correct the situation. Do they do it? Only in very rare instances.

The reason for our failure to keep promises we make to ourselves is obvious. In most cases, no one but ourselves knows of the promises, and we will not intentionally punish ourselves for breaking them.

I maintain that it is more important to keep the promises we make to ourselves than it is to keep those we make to others. We have to live with ourselves, and when we continually fail to do the things we intend to do, we lose our self-respect, and, if we cannot respect ourselves, it is expecting too much to look for respect from others.

Frequently a tinge of crimson will cross my face as I think of the hundreds, yes, perhaps thousands, of promises I have made to myself and never kept. And as I look back over those days, I recall that I didn't like myself as well as I might. Every time I learned of someone I knew making strides, I would remember the many times I promised myself to do the things which would help me to climb.

One Monday evening I was preparing to retire and, while removing my clothing, my mind flitted over the things which had transpired that day. Nothing of importance happened. It was just another day. Then, with slight embarrassment, I remembered the promises I had made to myself over the week-end: I would start the week by organizing my desk and make plans for the entire week. I would tackle the tough assignments first. I would spend a certain amount of time for self-improvement, etc., etc. These, however, were merely promises but, as usual, the week had started and none of them were kept. The legend about the straw which broke the camel's back was quite apropos to the manner in which I felt that night. For some reason, and fortunately so, I was thoroughly disgusted with myself—so much so that I went to bed with a feeling that it would be a wakeful night. As I realized how undependable I was, an unusual thought crossed my mind. "If a child continually disobeyed, I most likely would exert myself to find a remedy; yet I have never done anything to try to correct my disobedience to myself." An idea came! I decided that, for one week, I would keep every promise I made to myself. Before making it, however, I would carefully weigh it to make sure I could keep the pledge. This was not easy at first. Habit is a most powerful condition. I resolved to do certain things the following day, and when the next day arrived, was tempted to slide along and sidetrack the promise. But I stuck to my resolution. I actually forced myself to do the things I had laid out to do. By the end of the week I had made such strides—and felt so much more satisfied with myself—I determined to continue on the routine of self-discipline.

Do I work harder than I did before making such a resolution? No. In fact, I don't think I work quite as hard as I did. To give a concrete example: It had always been an effort to keep my desk orderly. Mail comes in, and after reading it, it is laid aside for further reference. Something is piled on that, which makes it as good as lost. Papers of various kinds come to my desk for attention. I lay them aside until some future time. The result? My desk was always a pile of miscellaneous items—most of which had been neglected. Later I would always find myself in the position of taking time to explain why this and that had not been taken care of. And, incidentally, my mind never was at ease when at the desk, because all of the mass would point accusing fingers at me, reminding me that here were many things crying for attention.

One of the first promises I made to myself, after the burst of determination, was to get my desk properly organized. It would have been easy to put that off, because when the time came to tackle the job, I knew I would uncover a multitude of things I should attend to. But I kept that promise. I buckled down and removed everything, one by one, and in doing so, would either put it away properly, or take care of whatever was to be done. It was not an easy job—but it is amazing how pleasant it became. Before I was half through I found a song in my heart as I saw a bit of order coming to my desk.

Regarding the desk, I had made another promise to myself—and that was to keep it clean; to care for everything the moment it came to me for attention. Do you know that my work was much simpler thereafter? And, best of all, my mind was more at ease. I could sit at my desk without inner embarrassment.

Here is another little weakness of human nature I have discovered: Many times, when starting a job, we will sit and think about it for many minutes before we start—sort of dreading the initial effort. And, of course, the longer we meditate thinking about a job, the more difficult it becomes in our imagination. It reminds me of the days I was afraid of cold water. I would visit the beach and for a long time play around the edge of the water trying to get courage to jump in. Poking a toe in the surf, the sensation of coolness would make me withdraw it in a hurry. I did such things until I got thoroughly disgusted with myself, and finally, in desperation, jumped in, merely to find how pleasant it was after the entire body had been submerged. With the tremendous satisfaction I was getting by keeping promises made to myself, it was not difficult to form a habit of starting new jobs at once before even taking time to consider how easy or difficult they might be. Naturally, at the end of the week, there would be considerable pride in reviewing the great many things accomplished.

Up to this point, it may seem I am urging my readers to become like machines—to work, relentlessly, from the moment of arising to time of retirement. This would be very far from the truth. In fact, I think rest and recreation are just as essential to a well-balanced life as work. I will go so far as to say that unless you do allow sufficient time for restful recreation, the work you do will lack quality. So, another promise you should make to yourself, and which you should keep, is to arrange your day's work so that you can have time to relax and rest. And, here is a promise I will make you! Living according to this new routine of self-discipline you will thoroughly enjoy your rest periods. You will enjoy them because your mind will be at peace and not confused with a myriad of promises you should have kept, but didn't.

So far I have been talking about self-promises in a general way; but right now, I want to bring up a promise you should make—and keep. It relates to the book in your hands this moment.

Undoubtedly your intentions were good when you obtained this book. You read or heard that it might prove of help to you, and you're reading it, perhaps in hope that it will help you. Your intentions are no doubt sincere and you intend to *try* the things suggested—to see what happens.

I have never forgotten the time when a very wise man gave me a bit of good advice. "I intend doing what you suggest," I told him. "Hell is paved with good intentions," he snapped, "start doing it now!"

We are all human and from childhood we fall into the pattern of following the lines of least resistance. We form —and live—according to habit patterns. Any change—no matter how trivial—means the formation of a new habit. Therefore it is so easy to think that you will do tomorrow the thing which you might—and should—be doing now.

The principles which will be covered in this book have been proved; not once or twice—but by thousands of people. Men and women in all walks of life have gained greater success, health and happiness through the application of these simple principles. Transformations which have taken place in the lives of men and women seem almost unbelievable. The principles as you will find them are given in a manner so simple your intelligence will tell you in no unmistaken terms that you, too, can climb to pinnacles of great height. So certain will you be that you can duplicate what others have done you will *intend* to do everything suggested.

This intention on your part will not be one of those which will be applied towards the pavement in Hades. It will forecast success, because it will be *backed by action.*

The story is told of the lad who visited the sage in search of wisdom. "Come with me, my lad," said the wise man, and without conversation, walked slowly toward a nearby lake. Reaching the shore of the lake the sagacious man, without hesitation, continued walking into the lake. Deeper and deeper became the water until it reached the lad's neck. His frightened eyes meant little to the sage as he continued until, finally, the water covered the boy's head. After a moment, the man of wisdom turned around and as informally walked to shore.

After reaching dry land, the kindly old gentleman wryly asked the boy: "When under water, what did you want more than anything on earth?" Not a moment was required for the lad to answer this question. "Air was all I wanted, sir," he gulped. "Well, my son," mused the patriarch, "in order to gain wisdom, you must want it as badly as you wanted air, when under water."

* * *

Before attempting the next chapter, whether that be a day, a week—or even longer—get yourself in the frame of mind whereby your determination is so great, you will not allow anything to stand between you and complete success so far as these principles are concerned.

It is not my intention to build within your mind a consciousness that hard labor will be involved in carrying through on the suggestions to be made. They will be simple, indeed, but since it is so easy to postpone the start of anything new, I want you to start right now in keeping all promises you make to yourself. There is something else I would like to say in connection with this new promise of yours. Along with your determination to keep the promise, build up an enthusiasm to go along with it.

There is a vast difference between the quality of work done as a duty and that which is done with enthusiasm. The enthusiasm is reflected in every phase of the job.

Passively reading this book will do a certain amount of good. To follow through on the suggestions in a matter-of-fact way will add to the good you will gain. But to *approach this work with unbounded enthusiasm* will bring a result far and beyond any concept of your present imagination.

The fine finish you admire on expensive furniture did not result from a mere application of a coat of varnish. Much preparatory work had to be done. The wood had to be properly treated through sanding, filling, priming, etc., before any of the finishing coats were applied.

These first two chapters are preparatory steps, laying the proper foundation so that you will be ready to accept and absorb life's golden secrets as they are revealed to you.

As I write these lines, I am approaching my mid-sixties. I have not been successful all of my life by any means. I passed the age of fifty before I began to understand the principles as are now being revealed to you—and, at the time of the revelation, I was not only without money, but heavily in debt. During my fifties, I made greater progress —by following the precepts of these fundamentals—than I had made in my first fifty years put together; and, please note, since passing the age of sixty, I have made greater

gains than I did in the fifties. With these secrets, and at
my present age, I would not fear being stranded in a
country where I would be unknown and without a friend
or a penny. I know that, without undue hardship, I could
rise again to a position of security and comfort.

I am not bragging about myself. I have not done anything, nor am doing anything, which you cannot do—and
in the pages to come, the secrets which enabled me to find
peace of mind and material security, will be unfolded to
you—and in a manner which you can use in making them
your very own.

These things are being told to you at this time to
arouse your imagination. I want you to see yourself as you
would like to be. Visualize the type of a life which would
spell complete happiness for you; then . . . follow a routine which will now be presented.

In Chapter One you began building a consciousness
which enabled you to see that you *can* be a success. I hope
you have been faithful—to yourself—by building on the
affirmation; I CAN be a Success.

Now, just as water in a receptacle on a range will come
to a boil as sufficient heat is applied, lay this book aside
for a few moments, walk up and down the floor, and with
chin out and fists clenched, declare to yourself: I *WILL*
be a Success.

Know that you WILL be a success because you will take
the steps which lead you to success.

Before bringing this chapter to a close, there is one
warning I must leave with you. Many times one will think
he is following this instruction when all he is doing is

wishing for success. Then he will feebly exclaim that the principles do not work because he has tried them.

If you can keep from doing so, do not read the next chapter for a day or two. Allow sufficient time to elapse to enable you to fix the thoughts given in this one, firmly in your mind.

If you have been longing for something for years and years, and suddenly found it would soon be yours, can you imagine your enthusiasm? You would be walking on air—in anticipation of the happiness to come. Great blessings are to come in your life through the application of these Golden Secrets, so be enthusiastic, *fervently enthusiastic* over the new life about to be yours.

I'll make a prediction! Twenty-four hours after you begin developing the consciousness that "I WILL be a Success" you will notice a great difference in the reflection which greets you when you look in the mirror. And, it will not end there. Friends will comment on the new YOU. asking you about the change they see in you.

In using the word "Success" I am referring to success in its broadest form—not merely success from the standpoint of money and material things—but success in life; success in love; peace of mind.

Please do not underestimate the importance of this chapter. If you have not literally reached the boiling point so far as enthusiasm is concerned, for your own good, read this chapter again.

You MUST gain tremendously from this book. I will not be content with any half way results. And, you won't let me (yourself) down, will you?

CHAPTER THREE

Your Life's Pattern

THE ANSWER TO all life's problems will be found within that mind and body of yours. *Do you want riches?* You have the key to untold wealth, although you may not have used it. *Do you want more friends—more personal power?* Right now—locked within the depths of your *Creative Mind* * is the secret which will make you a magnet, drawing people to you.

Do you want better health? You have within a direct contact with the source of all life.

Do you want happiness? It can be found in only one place—and that is within. As we progress, you will discover a new sense of happiness you never experienced before.

Have you ever described yourself as being "this way" or "that way"; such as: "I am musical," or "I am *not* musical?" Or, "I am lucky," or "I am *not* lucky?" Do you know *why* you are "this way" or "that way?" Whether or not you can accept it now, you will learn that the reason why you are "this way" and "that way" is because *you yourself*

---

* As you will learn in Chapter 5, the Subconscious Mind will be referred to as the Creative Mind.

34

decided to be that way. You do not believe it? That's all right. You will before you have read much further.

YOU ARE WHAT YOU THINK YOU ARE!

You might take issue with this statement. If you have been a failure, you might be saying: "I didn't fail because I *thought* of myself as a failure." But let's read on. You'll see.

One time, while traveling on a train between Chicago and New York, I sat opposite a man in the diner who appeared ill at ease. He timidly told me he had never been in a diner before and did not know how to order, and asked me if I would assist him. I was happy to do so. Then he told me why he was taking the trip.

He had been a letter carrier for many years. His work had not been easy—lugging a heavy mail bag day in and day out, in weather ranging from sweltering heat in the summer to the icy blasts of winter. On his route was a mail-order house which received large bundles of letters daily; most of them containing orders with money.

"Why can't I be in business and have a mailman bring important letters to me, instead of carrying them to others?" he asked himself. The answer came as he realized, that up to that moment, he had never seen himself as a business man. He prepared by studying a bit each evening, and later embarked on a business of his own. It had grown to a point where he was taking a trip to New York to purchase merchandise.

That man had been a letter carrier because he had *thought* of himself as a letter carrier. As soon as he changed the mental image of himself—that new image began to manifest itself in his affairs. *YOU ARE WHAT YOU THINK YOU ARE!*

In the middle west, an accident took the life of the husband of a very timid woman, leaving her and her two young daughters without visible means of support. This unhappy widow found that by drudging at least fourteen hours daily, doing housework for others, as well as looking after her own family, she could eke out an existence.

Whenever she would hear stories of the success of other women, she became more and more discontented with her own lot and gradually sank to lower depths of despondency. After carrying on without a husband for about two years, she was ready to give up. She had become reconciled to the thought of putting the children into an institution and taking a job as a domestic helper where she would have regular hours—and regular periods for rest and relaxation.

One day this sad woman happened to pick up a card bearing the thought: *You can do ANYTHING if you THINK you can.* "Oh yes?" she said to herself as she visualized her own plight. Then, after a few moments of sane reflection, she asked herself this challenging question: *Why can't I do the things I would like to do?* Almost as though an inner voice had whispered to her—she got the answer. It came to her clearly that the reason why she was in her predicament was because she had never seen herself as anything else.

Without realizing it, she began tapping the omnipotent power contained within all of us, and in less than three years she was living in Southern California, owned a business, and was able to take excellent care of her children.

Now then, this woman *had* been a timid household drudge because she had seen herself as such—but the moment she began seeing herself as a successful woman, her life began to change—to coincide with her new mental image. *YOU ARE WHAT YOU THINK YOU ARE!*

A salesman was getting very discouraged with his lot. He had been selling on a straight commission basis. His sales were small and not too frequent—a combination which meant unsatisfactory income. Each time he learned of a salesman pulling in a big order and making a large commission, he became still more disgruntled.

One day while Mr. A. (we'll call him) was eating a sandwich at a counter in a downtown restaurant, he saw one of the *bigshot* salesmen (and we'll call him Mr. B.) sitting at a table with a prospect, both of whom were enjoying a big, thick, luscious filet mignon. Mr. A. stared at Mr. B. several moments trying to figure out what Mr. B. had that *he* did not possess. Mr. A. knew that Mr. B. did not have a better education, because they both went to the same school and Mr. B. had not graduated, whereas Mr. A. had done so. What was the difference? *YOU ARE WHAT YOU THINK YOU ARE!*

Mr. A. reached the conclusion that he had been a small man because he had never visualized himself as anything else. On the other hand, Mr. B. had always seen himself as a top-flight salesman, booking large, profitable orders. The moment Mr. A. raised his sight, the moment he began seeing himself as an important salesman, his business began to grow—and within a year he had tripled his income.

YOU ARE WHAT YOU THINK YOU ARE! As I say

this, I am not implying that you like the condition in which you find yourself. No, you *would* like to be different, but you have remained as you are—because you have *seen* yourself *as you are.* The habits you have, which you would have liked to overcome, are with you, because you have not been able to see yourself without them. Perhaps your health is not better than it is, because you have never raised your vision to that point where you have *seen* yourself as radiantly healthy. You might not have achieved the success of life you had *wished* for, because you had not *seen* yourself as being successful. You have not reached a state of supreme happiness, because complete happiness has not yet become a part of your consciousness.

Planning Your New Life

You wouldn't start on a long journey without knowing where you were going. You have your road map well studied before you head for the open spaces. And, this is right—just as it should be.

You are learning life's golden secrets for the purpose of getting more out of life—to enable you to get what you want. But—*do you know what you want?* Amazingly few know what they do want. We are discontented, but when someone pins us down with the question: "Exactly what do you want?"—it is hard to give an answer.

Soon you will begin laying out your "road map" for your new life—which will take you to the goal of greater success, better health and more happiness. But, before you reach that point, it is necessary that you know the direction in which you wish to travel. So, as you continue, read with great care—and then follow instructions.

Since it is true that *YOU ARE WHAT YOU THINK YOU ARE,* from this day onward you will begin changing your mental image of yourself—in other words, you are going to begin seeing yourself as a *NEW YOU!* A personality radiantly magnetic; eminently successful and scintillating with Health and Happiness.

What Kind of a Life Do You Want?

If there were no barriers—and you could have anything you wanted—what would you want? Do you want more of the worldly goods? Would you like to have a modern home? A new automobile? A large wardrobe? Lots of money in the bank?

Do you want a better job? A business of your own? Do you want more power? To be looked up to in your community? To be a person of important affairs?

Do you want better health? Do you long for that glad-to-be-alive feeling? Would you like to be popular and have lots of worthwhile friends?

If your answer to any—or all—of these questions is yes, would it sound too good to be true should I tell you that to acquire them is well within the realm of possibility? Does this read like the story of Aladdin and his Magic Lamp? Perhaps, but truth is frequently stranger than fiction—and the ease with which we can get more out of life is so little understood, it is generally looked upon as fiction.

In San Francisco, a woman was just moving into a most palatial home. An electrician, who was connecting the meter, remarked: "It must be wonderful to be rich and live in a home like this.'' The new owner smiled sympathetically and replied: "I am not rich. Two years ago I had next to nothing, but an awakening I had, through learning life's golden secrets, all of this grandeur has come into being."

Daydreaming is usually discouraged, and is seldom advisable—but right now, for a while, *I want you to daydream*. Visualize the life you would *like* to have. Don't be afraid to be generous. *You will never get any more out of this life than you expect.* So, just as if living in the land of make-believe, imagine this chapter as your Magic Lamp —and that through it you will get what you want in life— then decide exactly what you *do* want.

In the opening lines of this book, I asked you to approach this work with an open mind; now I will tell you why. You are now about to learn a bit regarding the type of results which may be yours through the application of that which will be revealed in later chapters. To tell you that you may have the things you have wished for—but which you never expected were meant for you, would stretch your credulity to such an extent it would prove a handicap—and prevent the actual attainment of the many good things which may be yours.

As you advance—and begin to understand *why* the principles operate as they do—you will automatically eliminate any doubt which may be caused through previously conceived opinions.

Before proceeding further, there is an important statement I would like to make. What I am giving to you is no invention of mine. I am merely asking you to use basic laws and principles—which have been with us since the beginning of time. The only part I am playing is assembling them in such a manner as to make them readily understandable and applicable.

You might gaze at a giant transport airplane, and as the many tons of metal and other materials, along with human cargo, soar aloft, you may express amazement at what man has accomplished. But has it ever occurred to you that there really isn't anything new about an airplane? The metal from which it is built has been with us for countless ages, buried in Mother Earth. Even the fuel that propels the plane came from the earth. Really, the only thing new about an airplane is our knowledge of combining and assembling the materials; making that which you see so gracefully soaring above. This is true regarding the principles given to you herewith. They have always existed. The only thing new about them is the discovery of the personal power we may attain—when we make proper use of them.

Now then, if you were taking a trip, you would want to know just where you were going—before you started your trip, wouldn't you? Naturally. You would not load up your car and, with no destination in mind, start out. True, you might change your course from time to time after you once got under way, but at least, before you stepped on the gas, you would know about where you were heading for. I want you to assume the same attitude toward these golden secrets. I want you to determine in your own mind what it is you expect from them. Be specific! Crystallize in your mind exactly what you want to accomplish. What I will ask you to do now may seem strange, but, as you progress, you will understand the reason for doing so.

Obtain a blank book to be used as your *plan book*. You may obtain one at the stationery counter in any ten-cent store. Before writing anything down, meditate for a while and ask yourself this question: "If I could have anything I want, what do I want?" Think about it very seriously. Forget any limitations for the moment. Just picture yourself in a situation where you can help yourself to anything; money, house, car, better job—a business of your own. What would you take under such conditions?

How about your physical being? Are you enjoying radiant health? If not, think of the changes you would like in your physical body.

As your wants crystallize in your mind, write them down. Take a page and at the top label it, "Objectives for my physical being." Take a second page and label it, "Objectives for my possessions." And a third page which could be titled, "Objectives for my affairs."

On the page for your physical being, write down the changes you would like to have in that body of yours; a few of which might be such as:

> Reduce in weight
> Younger face and body
> More energy
> Overcome timidity
> Conquer bad habits
> Etc., etc., etc.

On the page for your possessions list the things which you believe would make you happy—and don't be afraid to be generous with yourself. You will never get dollars if you think in terms of dimes. This page may include such items as:

> Home of your own
> A new automobile
> A fine wardrobe of clothes
> A substantial bank account
> New range
> Washer and dryer
> Television
> Sewing machine
> Fine camera

When considering the page for your affairs, you may want to list such items as:

> A better job
> A business of my own
> Lots of friends
> The right husband—or wife
> A career in (name it, such as acting, writing, painting, music, law, medicine, architecture, etc.)

What I am about to suggest may seem a bit fantastic to you—but, be that as it may, I urge you to follow instructions. In later chapters you will learn why you are asked to do this—and how you put the forces of nature to work for you by doing so.

If a lawyer should notify you that a sizable estate had been left to you, and would give you a long list of all that was included in the estate; the various buildings, the furnishings, automobiles, etc., you would get a thrill each time you would read through the list, wouldn't you? As you would see each item, a picture would come to your mind of yourself—and family, enjoying that which was soon to be yours. This is the feeling you should have each time you review the items you are now placing on these lists. At least three times each day; morning, noon and evening—run through the lists from beginning to end. Do not look at the pages as though you were scanning an index of some kind. *Visualize* yourself as possessing each of the objectives and feel stimulated in anticipation of your possessing them.

There is a psychological foundation for this procedure. A bit later you will understand that by proceeding with this routine you are actually putting the forces of nature to work for you in making these objective realities.

There is one phase of this routine which will at once be apparent. Worry, if you will stop to think about it, is nothing more than holding mental pictures of *things you do not want*. This plan now being unfolded to you will train you to think in terms of things you *do* want. And, any psychologist worthy of the name, will tell you that to do this is a vital step toward acquiring that which you do want.

The executive of a local union, when following this study, made up a list consisting of 72 items. Within a year, he had crossed off over forty of them as having come into existence. One of the objectives was to become a good speaker. Now a good part of his work is addressing groups of members and he does so in a most forceful manner.

A woman who took up this study to overcome timidity, and who later became a top-notch insurance saleslady, said that she had made up a very long list—and that every item on it had been checked off. Some of the objectives which were included, she happily told me, were such that she felt reluctant about putting them down, because she could not feel there would be any likelihood of attaining them— yet, when they did come to pass, they did so in such a natural way, one would think they had always been expected.

I hope you will be very sincere in following through on the suggestions given in this chapter. The results you will obtain will be such that the securing of this book will prove to be one of the greatest investments you have ever made.

Allow at least three days to elapse before starting on your next chapter—and in the meantime keep your lists of objectives constantly before you.

You can always change your lists; take off items you have decided against—or add new items to the lists. Keep it right up to date.

CHAPTER FOUR

The Art of Relaxation

THIS SUBJECT IS included in this book—and in this position for a very sound reason. As you will learn later in this chapter, the mind absorbs knowledge much more readily while the body is relaxed than when tense. Therefore pay most careful attention to everything given in the next several pages—and hereafter, before approaching a new chapter—relax—thoroughly. You will enjoy your reading much more and gain far more from it.

Relaxation *is* an art. Most people realize the value of relaxation—yet it is difficult to find a person who can thoroughly relax at will.

First, know the truth of this statement: The body is *consuming* energy when it is tense—the body is *restoring* energy when it is relaxed. *Always remember this!* Naturally, in the performance of most of our work, we must use energy. That is why our internal laboratories are constantly converting much of the food we eat into energy. But, when we are working, when the body is tense, we are consuming energy at a rate faster than it can be generated. This means, we are drawing on our reserves. If we are living correctly—and relax as much as we should, we will have a sufficient reserve to carry us through to the next period of relaxation. If we don't relax as much or as thoroughly as we should, we begin to suffer from fatigue long before the close of the day. On the other hand, the fortunate individual who has truly learned to relax—is able to carry on and feel *fit as a fiddle* after hours of labor.

Sitting down or lying down does not necessarily mean you are relaxing. You can be just as tense sitting in a chair or lying in bed as you are while you work and, naturally, in both cases, you are *burning energy* instead of *storing* it.

Even though very few people know *how* to relax, it is not difficult to learn. It is not difficult to learn the rudiments of music, but it does take practice to become a musician. In this chapter I will show you *HOW to relax;* but you will not gain the good from this knowledge until, through practice, you acquire the habit of automatically relaxing—every time an opportunity presents itself.

Here is the key thought in this method of relaxation: *A HUMAN BEING IS A MIND WITH A BODY; NOT A BODY WITH A MIND.* We hear of a man owning a house; but do we hear of a house owning a man? Knowing that we are *MINDS* with bodies, we can understand now that the *MIND* is the *MASTER* and the *BODY* the *SERVANT.* We will also conclude, as we think more about relaxation, that it is just as much psychological as it is physiological.

Here is an experiment I want you to conduct *right now!* Before reading beyond this paragraph, sit in a comfortable chair and *TRY* to relax for just five minutes. I emphasized the word *TRY,* because that is just what it will be—a *TRY.*

All right, lay this aside until you have attempted to relax.

Now then, did you relax for five minutes? Do you feel any better? Probably you will say you don't feel a *bit* better than you did before—and some might even feel a bit worse. Do you know why? You were not relaxed because you *tried* to relax. This sounds queer until I make myself clear. You were using *will-power* to make yourself relax. Instead of causing you to relax, it made you more tense than you were before. As you know now, you burn energy while you are *tense,* which means you were not resting a particle during the five minutes of attempted relaxation. This is easy to understand, isn't it?

Now you have learned something else about relaxation. You have learned that your *will-power* is of little help so far as relaxation is concerned. To use *will-power* is the same as to use *force.* That body of yours is your servant and is willing and anxious to serve you—*without force.*

Here is another experiment: Hold out your right arm. Open and close the hands a few times. Now wiggle your fingers, one at a time. Move your arm up and down once or twice. You had no difficulty at all in doing any of these things, did you? *HOW* did you make those movements? By using *will-power? NO!* You had a *desire* backed by *faith;* the *desire* to move your hand or arm, backed by *faith in your ability to do so.* You didn't have to use *will-power* because you *knew* you could control the movements of your hand and arm, and you also *knew* your hand and arm would respond to the desires of our mind.

If you can control the movements of various parts of your body merely by expressing a thought, isn't it logical to assume that the muscles of your body will relax in response to a mental desire? *YES, THEY WILL.*

In time you can reach a state whereby you'll *automatically* relax the moment you sit down—but, until that state is reached, it will be necessary for you to develop a relaxation consciousness through a simple routine I give you in this chapter.

I am certain you have frequently heard the expression *"cat-nap,"* haven't you? And, you have noticed how quickly a cat drops off to sleep and also how refreshed it is—even after but a few minutes of sleep. Do you know *why?* A cat, the moment it lies down, will thoroughly relax from the tip of its nose to the end of its tail. Complete relaxation is conducive to sleep, and a short period of sleep, while thoroughly relaxed, is *more* refreshing than a much longer period when the body is tense.

* * *

Here is your routine for relaxation. It is suggested that you follow this procedure at least once each day—twice or three times if possible.

First, make yourself comfortable, either in bed, or on a chair. Next, without using any *will-power* whatsoever, begin sending relaxation thoughts to all parts of your body, and *know* that your muscles will respond—just as your hand and arm did a moment ago.

Begin with your left foot. Think of the toes and suggest to them that they relax—*knowing in your mind that they will relax.* Next suggest to your foot that it, too, relax. Instruct your ankle to relax; the calf of your leg—your knee; and right up to your body. Next, do the same with your right leg, starting with the toes and continuing on to the body.

Now take your arms, one at a time, starting with the fingers; then hand, wrist, and continue until you reach the body.

Next, relax your head, face and neck. Actually talk to each part—telling it to relax: *Throat relax! Chin relax! Neck relax! Etc.*

All right, now relax your torso, starting with the chest and continuing down through the region of the bowels.

In the beginning, it should take you from three to five minutes to go over the entire body. After you have followed this routine a few times, you will reach a point where you become so thoroughly relaxed, you will feel almost as though you have no body at all.

*　　*　　*

From now on, become relaxation conscious. Every time you sit down—check up on yourself to see if you are relaxed. If your hands and fingers are wiggling around—they are *not* relaxed. If your legs and feet are on the move, *they* are *not* relaxed. Talk to the various parts of your body. They all belong to you and will obey you.

If you will keep relaxation in your mind, you soon reach a point where you will relax every opportunity you have—without even thinking of relaxing. When you are on the bus or trolley—you can relax. Between jobs you can relax. You will find—after you have mastered the art of relaxation—you will be able to do *far more work* with *less fa-*

tigue. You will even find that you are getting far more enjoyment from your work than you did before.

* * *

I have been telling you a bit about the physical aspects of relaxation; let's think about the psychology of relaxation.

In this book you are learning that all thoughts held in the conscious mind are patterns which are accepted by the creative mind—and which later become manifest in the physical being.

Most people (and this might mean you) constantly say: "I can't relax." Such a statement or even such a thought is, in effect, an instruction to your creative mind to create a condition of tenseness within your being.

From now on, along with your routine of exercises—you will hold the correct mental pattern with such thoughts as: "I am completely relaxed," or "I have complete control of my physical being; when I am at ease, my body *is relaxed.*"

And, continuing with the psychological consideration of relaxation, permit me to say—that it is just as necessary to relax *mentally* as it is *physically*. In fact, it is *impossible* to relax *physically* unless you *are* relaxed *mentally*. If you have a mind filled with problems, when taking your relaxing exercises, decide that you will lay your cares aside for the time being and return to them later. Yes—you can do *just that*. And here is the interesting phase of this regime: when you return to your problems, they will not appear as big to you as before. Your period of relaxation has sharpened your vision; your judgment; your ability to fearlessly cope with your problems.

BETTER SLEEP THROUGH RELAXATION

"I sleep soundly all night, yet I am always tired when I wake up in the morning." Have you ever heard this expression? Permit me to say that one can sleep without being relaxed. And, when you are tense all night, you are not restoring energy, with the result that you are almost as tired in the morning as when you went to bed.

I can give you some simple rules which will enable you to go to sleep quickly, sleep peacefully, and awaken in the morning refreshed.

1. *Do NOT use will-power in trying to go to sleep. The more you WILL yourself to sleep—the wider awake you will become. After you have retired just realize how good it feels to be in a comfortable bed with your clothing removed—and DON'T CARE if you sleep or not. Yes, that is what I mean. Do not care about your sleep. You are comfortable and are resting.*

2. *Remove all the cares of the day from your mind. There is nothing you can do about them while you are in bed—so forget them for the period of sleep.*

3. *Go through the relaxation routine, starting with your toes and following through until you have covered your entire body—that is, if you can. It is more than likely you will be sound asleep before you finish.*

After a night of peaceful, relaxed sleep, you will find yourself arising in the morning with an abundance of energy. And, if you start the day well—it is quite likely to end well.

KEEP YOUTHFUL THROUGH RELAXATION

In learning to relax, do not forget the facial muscles. Most of the unpleasant expressions you find on faces were put there through tenseness. The verticle lines between the eyes are put there when you wrinkle your forehead while thinking or working. The so-called crow's feet at the corners of the eyes are put there by squinting. Hard lines are carved around the mouth through anger and a bad disposition.

A smiling face is a relaxed face. You have heard much about the value of a smile so far as personality is concerned. Now you know that smiling will also enhance your beauty. So, do not forget to have a *pleasant smile on your face,* while you practice your relaxing exercises.

BETTER HEALTH THROUGH RELAXATION

It would be possible to write a book of several hundred pages, outlining the many physical ailments and complications which can come to the person who is constantly tense. The list could include indigestion, poor circulation, heart trouble, headaches, etc. On the other hand, it is easy to understand how health will improve in every way—after we learn the art of relaxation.

EATING WHILE RELAXED

The only time one should eat is when thoroughly relaxed. If you are under a mental or physical strain when your meal time arrives—*skip your meal*. It will do far less harm to be hungry for a few hours than to eat when the mind and body are tense.

At this point, I might add a word or two about bad dispositions. It has been found that, as a rule, a person with a bad disposition suffers from many physical ailments. Do you know why this is true? Usually most fussing and quarreling is done during meals. The one with an unpleasant disposition will find fault with everything and everybody. Food taken in the system under such conditions can not digest properly, with the result that the many ailments associated with indigestion will be experienced.

A husband suffered constantly from indigestion, constipation, headaches, etc. His medicine cabinet was like a miniature drug store; filled with pills and tablets of all kinds. Medical aid had failed completely in helping this unhappy man. A psychologist, in studying his case, learned that he was the *bully* type husband—always giving vent to anger during meal time. He was *tricked* into a state of good humor at meal time by his wife, who cleverly invited a close friend of his to spend a vacation with them. After a period of two weeks of peaceful eating, his indigestion left him.

Mastering the Art of Relaxation will be worth many times the cost of this book. Definite advantages will become apparent to you as you prove your mastery over your being, through the ability to relax at will. You will:

THINK EASIER. Thoughts flow with greater ease when mind and body are relaxed.

THINK BETTER. A relaxed mind is one under

control; hence, a better quality of thought can be expected.

HAVE MORE ENERGY. Since relaxation helps you to store energy, you will be able to do more work, and better work, with less fatigue.

HAVE A BETTER DISPOSITION. Tenseness often will cause irritability.

KNOWLEDGE IS OF NO VALUE UNTIL YOU MAKE USE OF IT

Just knowing how to relax is not enough. You must transform that knowledge into experience, and the only way to do that is through practice. Here are a few suggestions, and for *your* sake, follow through on them. They are simple—yet vitally important.

1. Read this chapter through again *thoughtfully, and s-l-o-w-l-y.*

2. *Become relaxation conscious* * and think in terms of *"I CAN relax."*

3. Make it a point to go through the relaxation routine two or three times each day, and immediately after retiring. Do this until it becomes second nature for you to relax on each occasion when energy is not called for.

THE LAW OF GRAVITY WORKS FOR YOU!

Place a sack of flour in an upright position and it will soon bulge at the bottom. The law of gravity is at work. Human beings, from the time of birth, spend about two-

* We will learn more about this in our study of the Creative Mind which starts in a later chapter.

thirds of each 24 hours in an upright position—even when sitting. The law of gravity still works—and often the protruding "tummy" which we think of as being fat, is nothing more than drooping organs—prolapses— (a rather general female complaint).

The slanting board has been found to be a boon to both men and women. A few fifteen-minute periods daily on the slanting board will throw the law of gravity into reverse and cause the organs to fall back into their natural positions.

The slanting board is any board about 16″ in width and at least 6′ long. It is placed with one end resting on a chair, bed, couch—or any solid object approximately 16″ in height. Lie on this board—on your back—with your head down. Do so for periods of about 15 minutes at a time, one or two times a day.

The use of the slanting board is recommended only for those of normally good health. If you are not in good health, consult your doctor before making use of the slanting board.

SLANTING BOARD FOR BEAUTY! Would you like to have your face lifted? Well, the slanting board will do it for you, in a most satisfactory manner. If your face and neck are showing signs of age—what do you see? The result of the law of gravity. The skin has become soft and old man gravity has been pulling down. When on the slanting board, look at yourself in a hand mirror. Notice—with pleasure—how gravity is encouraging the tissue of your neck and face up into its youngest and most line-free state.

As the tissue—and muscles—drop back into place, gravity is also bringing an additional supply of blood to that region, nourishing and strengthening your tissue and muscle —making it natural for them to remain where they belong.

If you ever have occasion to use a beauty mask (beauty clay), the most ideal time is while reclining on the slant-ting board.

Before applying the beauty mask, lie on the slanting board a few moments in order to relax the muscles and tissue of the face and neck so they will naturally fall back to their original place. Then apply the preparation—following maker's instructions, of course.

Have you favorite radio programs? A good way to encourage regularity with the slanting board is to use it at a time when a favorite program is on the air. Listening to the radio while on the board will establish regularity of its use. In fact, when it is time for your program, you will automatically think of the slanting board.

SLANTING BOARD FOR HEALTH. The fluoro-scope reveals an amazingly high percentage of people with drooping colons. This is another evidence of the work of the law of gravity. And, with so many people affected with drooping colons, it is little wonder that there are so many people suffering from internal sluggishness—constipation.

The slanting board will throw the law of gravity into reverse and cause it to work for you—instead of against you. While using the board to relieve constipation, it is suggested that you gently massage the intestinal region with your hands, and, also, draw your stomach in as far as possible.

SLANTING BOARD FOR RELAXATION. In the beginning of this chapter you learned the value of relaxation. You will find your slanting board a great help in connection with relaxation. It is not at all difficult to relax while on the slanting board. So, you can consider that, while you are on the slanting board, you are not only helping to promote health and beauty—but you are also helping nature to restore lost energy through relaxation.

SLANTING BOARD FOR BRAIN WORKERS! When mentally tired from studying and thinking, you will find that a few moments on the slanting board will rest your brain so that you may resume your work with a clearer mind. Once a brain worker forms the habit of using the slanting board, he will find himself capable of far more—and better—mental work.

EXERCISING ON THE SLANTING BOARD! If you are following any routine of physical exercise—either for reducing or body building, you will be amazed to find how much more effective your exercises will be when done on the slanting board—with your feet much higher than your head. With all of your organs in their proper place, through the law of gravity, it is easy to understand that your exercising will develop the strength to keep your organs where they belong.

HOW TO MAKE A SLANTING BOARD! The simplest way to make a slanting board is to take two pieces of one-inch lumber (pine), eight inches wide and six feet long. These can be fastened together with three cleats; two of them 2 inches wide by 16 inches long, and one of them 2 inches wide by 24 inches long. Screw a 16 inch cleat on each end, and the 24 inch cleat in the center allowing 4 inches to protrude on each side, to act as handles. For comfort, you can upholster one side by attaching a thin layer of cotton over which a covering of durable cloth is added. Material similar to that which is used for slip covers will prove very satisfactory. If you intend using the slanting board for exercising, it will be well to fasten a strip of web material on one end. Allow enough slack in the web to permit the feet to be slipped under while exercising.

After reading a chapter in this book, it would be a splendid idea to relax on the slanting board for a few moments and reflect over that which you have read. You will find it well worthwhile.

CHAPTER FIVE

Your Mental Power House

IT IS SUGGESTED that, as you start this chapter—which will be one of the most important ones in the book—you relax thoroughly. First make yourself comfortable; then relax—mentally and physically.

Be certain that there are no annoying thoughts or problems on your mind which might be confronting you.

Mentally review the first chapter in which you introduced yourself to you. Think of the objectives you listed in Chapter Three, and sense a feeling of happiness—as you realize you are taking steps to bring them into being. Then—recall what you learned regarding relaxation—and make certain you are fully relaxed right now. After you have done this, you are ready to proceed with Chapter Five.

In observing an arch, have you ever noticed the wedge-shaped stone in the center—which appears to be providing the bulk of the strength to hold all stones in their place? That important stone is called the *KEYSTONE*. In fact, the *KEYSTONE* is often used as a symbol; representing a great binding force.

I like to think of this chapter as the *KEYSTONE* of your course of *CREATIVE PSYCHOLOGY*. Although every chapter is vitally important, from now on, most everything you learn will be based upon the facts which will be revealed in the next few pages. So, read thoughtfully. *Think* about it as you read. A workman might acquire an elaborate outfit of tools, but unless he has learned what they were for, and how to use them, they would prove of little value to him. This is true with these principles. Merely reading about them is not enough.

You must *understand them*. Just reading and trying to remember these suggestions will make them boring to you. But *understanding* the thoughts as given—makes each new chapter a thrilling adventure.

All right, now we take up a subject which has proved to be quite a controversial one among psychologists and metaphysicians. We are going to consider the various departments of *MIND*.

Some psychologists and metaphysicians consider the *MIND* as being three-fold: the *conscious, subconscious* and *super-conscious MIND*. The majority of them think of the *MIND* as being two-fold: the *conscious* and the *subconscious*. Then we will find a certain minority—who claim there is but one *MIND*.

Many branches of religious thought will refer to part of the mind as *DIVINE MIND—CHRIST MIND—GOD MIND—COSMIC MIND;* etc., etc.

I believe that *ALL MIND is GOD MIND*. It all belongs to *GOD*—regardless what your interpretation of *GOD* might be. So, although I will not refer to the mind hereafter as *GOD MIND,* that will be implied.

Regardless who might be right—whether it be a single mind, a two-fold mind—it makes no difference in our consideration of it and how we may tap its vast power.

For all intents and purposes, the mind can be considered as *dual* in its nature; and all of the benefits are within the realm of attainment for those who will follow the suggestions contained in *this* and later chapters.

In our consideration of mind, we think of it as being dual in its nature. You may think of it as a single mind with *two departments*—or *two associated minds,* as you wish. The common names for the two minds are the conscious or objective mind; and the subconscious or subjective mind. Hereafter I will refer to the two minds as: *CONSCIOUS* and *CREATIVE* (subconscious).

Since my first insight into the mind and how it operates, I have never been happy with the word "subconscious" as applied to the mind. The prefix "sub" is associated with anything which is under, below, beneath. We do not think of a sub-station as being of the same relative importance as the main headquarters.

Our study of *CREATIVE PSYCHOLOGY* will teach us that the portion of mind, heretofore known as the *subconscious mind,* is the real seat of intelligence and is our *GREAT RESERVOIR OF POWER.*

The benefits which you will gain from this course will come as a result of the new use to which you put this great mind. Therefore, in this course, you will learn much regarding the *CREATIVE MIND*—and how it works *with* you and *for* you.

In my descriptions I will refrain from getting technical. Should you later gain a desire to make a more comprehensive study of the mind, you undoubtedly will find it interesting—and profitable—to do so; but you will find also that, by making proper use of the knowledge which you gain from this work, you will reap rewards far beyond your present expectations.

In this chapter we discover what the two minds are, and as we proceed we will learn *how* they operate and how we may use them in bringing success, better health and happiness to ourselves and to our loved ones.

Your *CONSCIOUS MIND* is used for your *conscious* thinking and reasoning. When you decided to read this book the thought was prompted by your *CONSCIOUS MIND*. If you decide to go out for dinner, go to a show, or take a trip, all such thoughts emanate from your *CON-SCIOUS MIND*.

Your *CREATIVE MIND* controls all of the involuntary operations of the body, such as: *beating of the heart, the circulation of the blood, breathing, etc.*

Here is a fact which I want you to remember! The *CONSCIOUS MIND* is the *MASTER,* the *CREATIVE MIND* is the *SERVANT*. After having been told that the *CREATIVE MIND* is the seat of *INTELLIGENCE* and *POWER,* you might think it inconsistent to now read that the *CREATIVE MIND* is subservient to the *OBJECTIVE MIND,* but it is not at all inconsistent. The seat of power is in an army, yet, this mass of power comes under the direction of a single individual—the *GENERAL*.

The forces of our *CREATIVE MINDS* can enable us to climb to great heights, or can make us descend to the depths of despair. The power of water gives us a good illustration as compared to the forces of the mind. We have seen cities wiped out through floods, where a great many lives were lost, and thousands of people left homeless. This is the power of water *uncontrolled*. On the other hand, Hoover Dam, with its man-made lake, has made many thousands of desert acres tillable and productive, and is furnishing all of Southern California with electric current at an extremely low rate. This is the power of water *controlled*.

Let me give you a very simple illustration which will show you the relative position of both—your *CONSCIOUS* and your *CREATIVE MINDS*.

We will use a large organization for this example. To keep it simple, we will think only of the president as *owner of the factory*—and his general manager as *managing it*. The president, as you know, does all the *planning* for his factory. He decides on *what is to be manufactured,* and *HOW* it shall be manufactured. He passes his instructions down to the general manager, whose duty it is to carry out the instructions. At times, the general manager might not agree with the president, and may argue with him, but if the president should insist on having his way, it is the duty of the general manager to follow instructions.

All right, let us consider the body as a large institution. We will think of the *CONSCIOUS MIND* as the *PRESIDENT* and the *CREATIVE MIND* as the *GENERAL MANAGER*. There is one important difference, however. You will recall that I said the *GENERAL MANAGER* of a *FIRM* might disagree with the *PRESIDENT* and argue with him. Well, this is *NOT* true with the *CREATIVE*

MIND. It accepts all instructions as final and proceeds to follow them—*EXACTLY* as given.

Should the president of a factory desire a change made in the design of a product being manufactured. he will first create the new design of the product in his own mind. He will then give this new design to the general manager, and it will not be long before the product of the factory will bear the new design.

This same thing happens within the physical being. If the *CONSCIOUS MIND* holds to a certain thought, the *CREATIVE MIND* takes the thought as an instruction, and proceeds to make it manifest in the being and affairs of the individual.

Now then, here is something else I want you to remember! The president of a company will confine his planning to *constructive* changes to be made. No one would think of a president *intentionally* making changes which he knows would make his product *inferior*. It is ridiculous to even assume such a thing. The reason he is president is because he is capable of guiding his business in a constantly upward course. Should he prove incompetent, he either loses his position or wrecks the business.

As soon as we learn the *faithfulness* of our general manager, or *CREATIVE MIND,* and the tremendous reservoir of *POWER* at its constant command, we will see to it that nothing but *constructive* instructions are given to it by the president, or *CONSCIOUS MIND*. We will know that every time we maintain a negative or *destructive* thought, such as: "I am not feeling well," "I am getting old," "I cannot succeed," etc., we are actually asking our general manager, or *CREATIVE MIND,* to create such a condition in our beings, or in our affairs. We will also know that the opposite is true. Each time we hold to a positive or *constructive* thought, such as: "I am a Success," "I am gaining in strength," "I am gaining in Personal Power," etc., we are giving definite instructions to our general manager or *CREATIVE MIND* to create such conditions in our affairs or in our beings.

In the beginning of this chapter I told you I would not enter into any technical discussion as to why these things are true; it would not help you a particle toward the attainment of your objectives. It would mean that you have to wade through page after page of laborious reading, and in the end not be much better off than you are otherwise. If you should find an urge to study the technical side of this subject, fine; but it is not essential in order to gain great benefits from this work.

What I have attempted to do is to take the mass of material I have accumulated during many years and produce for you a short-cut into the realm of greater *Personal Power, Success and Happiness.* In this connection I might ask you two questions. First: Can you give an accurate description of an internal combustion engine, why and how it operates? Second: Do you drive an automobile? Unless you are an engineer, your answer to the first question will probably be "no." It is more than likely that your answer to the second question will be "yes." If you drive an automobile, you are successfully operating an internal combustion engine, whether you know what one is or not. This thought is probably new to you, yet it is true. If you had to become a trained engineer in order to operate an automobile, you might not have any desire to learn to drive. You will therefore understand—and appreciate—why I will not attempt to make a psychologist of you in order to enable you to use the great power of your mind.

All right, let us return to our discussion of the *CONSCIOUS* and the *CREATIVE MIND.* I have another illustration which will help you to understand the relationship between the *CONSCIOUS* and the *CREATIVE MIND.*

Have you ever visited a large printing plant and watched the operation of the linotype machine? You were amazed, I am sure, if you did so. You would see the operator press a key in the keyboard, which looks very much like the keyboard of a typewriter. The moment he does so, thousands of parts of the huge machine appear to come to life. You will see the matrix, or mould, drop down from above; it will move along to the casting portion of the machine, where it will be cast into type; then a large arm will reach down, pick up the matrix, and carry it back to the compartment where it came from. Sounds like magic, doesn't it?

Should the linotype operator touch the key marked "e", you would not expect to see the letter "f" or "g" made into the type "e". No. You would know that touching the "e" key will give you nothing but the letter "e" in type form. Well, this is true in our *mental* mechanism. We cannot press the mental key: "I am ill", and find the *CREATIVE* mechanism responding by making you well. Have I made myself clear? I am certain that, as you think about it, you will more fully understand.

I might give you still another illustration which will be

more readily understood. Since most of you operate an automobile, let us refer to one for a moment. When you wish to start the car, what do you think of? Do you think of the battery supplying current to the starter, and the generator making current to replace that which you use? Do you think of the distributor sending current to the right spark-plugs for the spark which will ignite the compressed mixture of air and gas? Do you think of the explosion taking place in the cylinders, furnishing power to the pistons? And the transmission gears? And the differentials? Etc.? No! You merely think of the ignition switch and the starter.

When you want to steer your car, do you think of all the mechanical details? For instance: the gears attached to your steering column, and the intricate mechanism which actually turns the wheels? No! You merely think of turning your steering wheel to the left or right. You instinctively know that all of the various parts will automatically respond to your touch of the wheel. When you turned the steering wheel to the right, was there ever any doubt in your mind as to the direction in which the car would go? You did not wonder if it would go to the right or to the left, did you? You knew that if you turned the wheel to the right, the car would turn to the right—and you would be correct.

Now I ask you a question, the answer to which will be more obvious to you than it *would* have been, had I asked it before you progressed this far. Is there any wonder why people *lack PERSONAL POWER, SUCCESS* and *HAPPINESS,* when they are always *THINKING* that they lack it?

In a later chapter you will learn that the *CREATIVE*

MIND has reasoning faculties, just as the *CONSCIOUS MIND;* but with this difference: The *CONSCIOUS MIND* can search for facts on which to build its reasoning. The *CREATIVE MIND* does its reasoning exclusively with the thoughts handed down by the *CONSCIOUS MIND*—whether they are facts or not.

Those who have given little or no thought to the *CREA- TIVE MIND* might feel that, in comparison to the *CON- SCIOUS MIND,* it is inconsequential indeed. Nothing could be more untrue. The reverse is absolutely right. The diagram will give you a fair idea of the relative size of both minds. This might at first seem a bit inconsistent, especially since we learn that the *CONSCIOUS MIND* is the *MASTER* and the *CREATIVE MIND* the *SERV- ANT.* But power, as has been demonstrated by the atom, is not a matter of size. The war taught us that the smallest thing was the most powerful: the atom. Compare the size of man with the giant locomotive and train which it pulls—*infinitesimal*—*yet,* the hundreds of tons of steel and human cargo are under the control of one man. In this comparison you know that, as well as controlling the train, he must control his own leadership—because a wrong move on his part could easily wreck the train. From now on, as you study this work, you will realize that the tremendous forces of your *CREATIVE MIND* are under the complete jurisdiction of your *CONSCIOUS MIND;* and when you are holding positive, constructive thoughts, this *MIGHTY POWER* is working toward your good, and that negative, destructive thoughts cause havoc within your being and affairs.

From now until you start on your next chapter, you are

going to work on a routine of *re-education* of the *CREATIVE MIND.*

Psychologists have found, through the study of countless thousands of cases, that 98% of all people have minds which lean on the negative side. This explains the reason why there are so few leaders. If you will compare the go-getter with the ne'er-do-well, you will find that the difference is not physical; it is not a matter of education; the *basic* difference is in the way they *think.* One will think in terms "I can", the others in terms of "I can't".

It is a bit early for you to fully understand the reason in back of the exercise I will give to you, but, whether you understand it or not, even whether you believe in it or not, I ask that you faithfully follow the suggestion below.

Every time you think of it, from the time you wake up in the morning, until you go to sleep at night, say to yourself, several times: "I'M FILLED WITH POWER— I'M FILLED WITH POWER—I'M FILLED WITH POWER," etc. If you are walking down the street, repeat it to yourself, in rhythm with your step. Do not miss an opportunity of practicing this exercise. You will notice a definite uplift every time you do. Remember now, not once, but many times. If you are by yourself, say it out loud. You might even make up a little tune and sing it: *I'M FILLED WITH POWER—I'M FILLED WITH POWER—I'M FILLED WITH POWER!*

One man, who had reached the depths of despair through financial reverses, changed his entire life merely through following this routine. After a few days of developing his *AWARENESS* of his power, he started to climb and had soon reached heights greater than he had ever known before. *FOLLOW THROUGH* with this exercise and, by the time you start on the next chapter, you will be amazed to discover the new spirit developing within you.

If you were shown a new machine and told of many wonderful things it would do, you would be interested, I am sure. But you, yourself, would not be able to get much from the machine without knowing how to use it. Merely knowing what it will do is not enough. You must have instructions how to use it, so that you can make it work for you.

You have been told much about the *CREATIVE MIND,* which is the real seat of intelligence and power. But, merely knowing that you *HAVE* a *CREATIVE MIND* is not enough. You must know how to tap this source of power—and how to make proper use of its vast intelligence.

Let us therefore begin by considering the intelligence of the *CREATIVE MIND,* and as you continue you will realize that the intelligence you might feel you have *CON-SCIOUSLY* is nothing at all compared with the intelligence continually manifested by your *CREATIVE MIND.*

Do you *CONSCIOUSLY* direct your breathing? Do you *CONSCIOUSLY* look after the beating of your heart? The circulation of your blood? Do you realize that within your being is a chemical laboratory *more perfect* than man has ever created? This laboratory selects from the food you eat, the vitamins, minerals and other elements necessary for blood, bone, tissue and energy. Do you *CON-SCIOUSLY* direct the operations of this laboratory?

During every twenty-four hours, tissue is wearing out

and is replaced by new tissue which has come into being. Do you *CONSCIOUSLY* construct the new tissue to replace the old, worn-out tissue?

The answer to all of these questions is: "NO!" You could not in a lifetime acquire intelligence enough, *conscious intelligence,* to handle any of these operations. Furthermore, your *CONSCIOUS MIND* can think only of *one thing at a time,* whereas all of the operations mentioned above, and thousands, yes, *millions* more, are proceeding simultaneously. An intelligence *must direct* them. It is the intelligence of your *CREATIVE MIND.*

It might be argued that the functions of the *CREATIVE MIND* already mentioned are *instinctive.* This could be, but it has been established that, in addition to the directing of all the involuntary operations of the body, the *CREATIVE MIND* has reasoning faculties. Yes, it can —and *does reason independently* of the *CONSCIOUS MIND.*

Have you ever used a fireless cooker? As you know, it is a cooking utensil capable of retaining stored heat for a period of time—sufficient to cook a meal without fire. To use a fireless cooker, you heat an element, put your food in the proper receptacle, close it tightly, and the heat will usually remain in this fireless cooker long enough to cook the food placed therein.

You can use your *CREATIVE MIND* in a way much similar to the use of the fireless cooker. If you have a problem you can submit it to your *CREATIVE MIND,* and while your *CONSCIOUS MIND* is thinking of other things, the *CREATIVE MIND* will, through reasoning, work on your problem, and later return the solution to you through your *CONSCIOUS MIND.* Soon you will realize that you *can* put your *CREATIVE MIND* to work, solving problems and making decisions for you.

Here is a truth which is probably new to you. *YOU RE NOT GOOD AT ANY WORK UNTIL YOUR CREATIVE MIND TAKES OVER.*

Do you use a typewriter? Do you type *consciously?* You may think so; but if you're good, you do not. When you first learned to type, you *did* type *consciously.* That was the time when you had to pick your way along, looking for this letter and that letter, etc. But, as you practiced, your *CREATIVE MIND* took over and now you type rapidly— as your *CREATIVE MIND* directs your fingers.

Do you drive a car? Do you do it *consciously?* When you first started to drive *you did*—and you were a poor driver. You had to direct each movement *consciously.* To stop the car, you'd think: "I disengage the clutch, take my foot off the accelerator, and apply it to the service brake." It takes time to reason out all of those operations *consciously,* with the result that many times you would have an accident because you did not work fast enough. After you had driven a while, your *CREATIVE MIND* assumed the job of driving, and you became a good driver. If you had to stop suddenly, you did all necessary things rapidly, and without *conscious* directing.

Are you musical? Can you play the piano? Do you do so *consciously?* When you first started to learn to play, you *did* so *consciously.* But as you practiced, your *CREATIVE MIND* accepted the responsibility and you became a good musician. As your eyes follow the notes, your *CREATIVE MIND* directs your fingers—and without *conscious thought.*

Do you write? Do you do so *consciously?* If so, you have not reached the stage of really being good. After you have gained the consciousness that you can write, after a theme has been evolved, your *CREATIVE MIND* will develop the story—and dictate it to your *CONSCIOUS MIND,* as you apply it to paper.

Do the good lecturers do their work *consciously?* If they had a talk memorized and reeled off like a phonograph, it would not be interesting at all. A good lecturer *knows* the subject on which he wishes to talk—and while talking —the continuity of thought is fed into his consciousness from his *CREATIVE MIND.*

You will learn more of the *WHY* and *HOW* of these things as you continue, but right now I have just cited a few illustrations to convince you of the *reasoning power—* and *intelligence—*of the *CREATIVE MIND.*

You *are* learning that your *CREATIVE MIND* is the seat of *POWER* and *INTELLIGENCE.* You *have* learned that, in size, your *CONSCIOUS MIND* is diminutive— compared to your *CREATIVE MIND.* But, notwithstanding this fact, your *CONSCIOUS MIND* is the *MASTER* and your *CREATIVE MIND* the *SERVANT.*

It is important that you fully appreciate the value of this truth. Those who are not getting the most out of life are the ones who are *SERVANTS* instead of *MASTERS* of their *CREATIVE MINDS.*

Fire can be your master or your servant. Fire can cause all kinds of destruction—when *uncontrolled.* But it can furnish light, heat and power when *controlled.*

Your CREATIVE MIND, when controlled, will bring to you *SUCCESS, BETTER HEALTH* and *HAPPINESS.*

When uncontrolled, it can cause *HARDSHIP, POV-ERTY, POOR HEALTH* and *MISERY*.

The object of this work is to teach you to *USE* your *CREATIVE MIND,* instead of being swayed by it. And *MASTERY* of the *CREATIVE MIND* is *not* difficult. The important thing is to become *AWARE* of its power, and to *KNOW* it is subject to your *COMMANDS*.

Right at this point, I suggest that before you proceed you turn back to Page No. 1 of this chapter and re-read everything up to this paragraph. Then, before you read further, reflect thoroughly over what you have read. Become fully *AWARE* of what you have learned—to the effect that your best work is done through your *CREATIVE MIND*. Then, as you begin to realize the tremendous reservoir of power contained within the *CREATIVE MIND*—rejoice to know that it is your *SERVANT—NOT* your *MASTER*. Yes, you have at your command a source of power which is ever ready to carry you to great heights of *SUCCESS* and *SUPREME HAPPINESS*. Now then, after you have followed this suggestion, you may continue.

The next point I wish to impress on your mind is your *CREATIVE MIND* does *NOT* take the initiative. *YOU* must press the button.

You might have a very expensive camera, one capable of making the finest photographs; but you must *PRESS* the *BUTTON*. The camera will not take pictures by itself.

You might have a fine motor car, but it will not run by itself. You must *DRIVE* it. You might have a splendid lighting system, but in order to get light *YOU MUST TURN ON THE SWITCH*.

These illustrations apply to your *CREATIVE MIND*.

Notwithstanding the fact that you have all of this power and intelligence at your command, you must make the *COMMAND* in order to cause your *CREATIVE MIND* to function for you.

Your Creative Mind Follows Your Instructions!

How do you instruct your *CREATIVE MIND?* The answer to this question is so simple, it is hard to accept. And, it is *understanding* the answer to this question which will enable you to get the greatest good from this course of study. Your *thoughts are instructions.* Remember that!

Now then, read the following paragraphs slowly and thoughtfully—they are so *vitally important!*

Your *CREATIVE MIND* is in charge of your entire physical being. Every organ in your body operates under the direction of your *CREATIVE MIND.*

The *THOUGHTS* you hold in your *CONSCIOUS MIND* are accepted as *INSTRUCTIONS* by your *CREATIVE MIND,* which acts accordingly. If you hold gloomy thoughts, your *CREATIVE MIND,* without argument, accepts such thoughts as instructions and proceeds to surround you with a feeling of gloom.

If you hold happy thoughts, your *CREATIVE MIND* accepts *them as instructions*—and proceeds to surround you with a feeling of joy and happiness.

If you hold thoughts of failure or poverty, your *CREATIVE MIND* will create an atmosphere of failure and poverty. There will be a lag in your step. Your eyes will be listless. There will be a whine in your voice. You will be all set to attract further failure and poverty.

In a later chapter you will learn that our bodies radiate either negative or positive vibrations, and that we actually *BROADCAST* our feelings to others. Right now we are considering merely the physiological aspect of thought.

If you hold thoughts of success and abundance, your *CREATIVE MIND* will create an atmosphere of *SUCCESS* and *ABUNDANCE*. You will have a spring in your step, a gleam in your eye, a quality in your voice, which will inspire confidence.

You might be interested in learning when this *great truth* dawned upon me.

I was operating an advertising agency in New York, and due to conditions beyond my control, my firm became heavily in debt—$30,000 in the red, to be exact. I had put every cent of my personal funds in the business, in an attempt to save it, but it seemed to be beyond control. Two of the many creditors had already started suit and the others were getting very uneasy.

For days I had to force myself to go to the office, because from the time the doors opened until I would leave at night, I would face the same thing—creditors phoning, asking for money. One morning, while I was waiting for breakfast and, incidentally, dreading my journey to the office, my mind reverted to some of the men who were making a big success of their businesses. I asked myself what they had *I did NOT have*. It was not physical, that was certain. It was not educational, because I knew of many who had had less training and experience than I had. As I pondered over this thought, I realized that the only difference between those at the top and those who couldn't make the grade, was a matter of consciousness. Those at the bottom were there because they could not see themselves anywhere else.

Almost as a ray of sunshine breaking through the clouds, the dark atmosphere of doubt began to leave me. Instead of dreading going to my office, as I had up to a few minutes before, I suddenly became anxious to do so. I hurriedly ate my breakfast and hastened to the bus.

Upon reaching the office, I asked my bookkeeper for a list of accounts payable, and I instructed her to get each creditor on the phone, one by one, until I had talked to all of them. And I started with the largest creditor first. The president of that firm came on the wire and I asked him to bear with me a bit longer, that I could make good on every cent I owed. His first question was: "Have you landed some good business?" My answer was: "No, but I have gained something more important, a new spirit." He replied: "I believe you have. I can detect it in your voice. Yes, I will help you."

Creditor after creditor was contacted, and all down the line the same spirit of cooperation was displayed.

Now then, with this new spirit, I not only allayed drastic action on the part of my creditors, but I went after new business with a success attitude, which enabled me to pay off every creditor within a period of a year.

That *CREATIVE MIND* of yours is at your service right now, obeying every *THOUGHT-INSTRUCTION* you give it. As you read on you will learn how to direct your *CREATIVE MIND* toward the attainment of *specific* objectives, whether those relate to success, better health, or happiness. But right now I want to suggest a routine for you to practice between now and the time you start on your next chapter.

There is a psychological truth to the effect, that *MOTION CREATES EMOTION.* The explanation of this is, if you go through certain motions a sufficient number of times, they create a habit pattern, and will become a part of you.

If you repeat a thought often enough, even though you might have difficulties in accepting it wholeheartedly at first, in time that thought will become effective. If you have trouble in believing this, the next time you are feeling low, relax, and for a few minutes say to yourself many times: "I AM HAPPY!" "I AM HAPPY!" "I AM HAPPY!" You will soon find the cloud of gloom fading away.

All right, from now on I want you to spend just a few minutes each morning and each evening with a pencil and paper, writing down the truths you want to make a part of your consciousness. The first thing you must do is to have *absolute faith in yourself;* faith that you can become successful, popular, radiantly magnetic, both in personality and in health.

As one of the affirmations, write at least twenty times, morning and evening: "I HAVE FAITH IN MYSELF!" The morning is a very important time, because during the day your *CREATIVE MIND* will be working on that thought—making it manifest in your actions. The evening is even *more* important. The *CREATIVE MIND* never sleeps, so putting thoughts in your *CREATIVE MIND* at night of such positive nature, means that, while your *CON*

SCIOUS MIND sleeps, your big reservoir of power and intelligence is making that condition of faith a reality.

If financial success is one of your objectives, with your pencil and paper, both morning and night, write such affirmations as: "I WILL BE A SUCCESS." Do not write this statement once, but many times. And keep it up morning after morning and evening after evening: "I WILL BE A SUCCESS." Do it at least until you take up your next chapter.

If you are not satisfied with your health, write down some positive statement regarding your health, such as: "I AM GAINING IN HEALTH AND STRENGTH."

If you have been morbid and blue, make use of this means of transposing your negative thoughts into cheerful ones. Try such written thoughts as: "I AM HAPPY!" "I AM HAPPY!" "I AM HAPPY!" etc.

In addition to these written exercises, form the habit of making positive declarations to yourself. Whenever you find a worry-thought entering your mind, chase it out with a *positive* thought.

Were it not for the many gauges on the instrument panel of your automobile, you would constantly damage your car. Not knowing when the radiator was dry would cause you to neglect adding water, allowing your engine to overheat. Burned-out bearings would result from inadequate oil. Your gas tank would often run dry. But the instruments before you guide you in doing the things you *should* do—*when* you should do them.

We cannot overestimate the *power* of thought. Its force is comparable to fire; it can prove destructive when uncontrolled; or constructive when controlled.

Negative thoughts are conducive to gloom, sorrow, misery, poor health, poverty. Positive thoughts are the forerunners of good health, prosperity and happiness.

If we could *see* thoughts, if we could have a gauge which would indicate the trend of our thoughts, we would be on guard seeing to it that no negative, destructive thoughts shall enter our minds.

Keep the following diagram as a symbol. Retain a picture of it in your mind. Each time a negative thought tries to gain entrance to your mind, visualize the needle leaning toward the red, or negative side, and know that the thought will cause you injury. Then you will at once reverse your thinking, moving the needle back to the *happy, prosperous* side.

Thot-o-meter

NEGATIVE   **POSITIVE**

WERE it not for the many gauges on the instrument panel of your automobile, you would constantly damage your car. Not knowing when the radiator was dry would cause you to neglect adding water, allowing your engine to overheat. Burned-out bearings would result from inadequate oil. Your gas tank would often run dry. But the instruments before you guide you in doing the things you *should* do; - *when* you should do them.

We cannot overestimate the *power* of thought. Its force is comparable to fire; - it can prove destructive when uncontrolled; - or constructive when controlled.

Negative thoughts are conducive to gloom, sorrow, misery, poor health, poverty. Positive thoughts are the forerunners of good health, prosperity and happiness.

If we could *see* thoughts; - if we could have a gauge which would indicate the trend of our thoughts, - we would be on guard seeing to it that no negative, destructive thoughts shall enter our minds.

Keep this diagram as a symbol. Retain a picture of it in your mind. Each time a negative thought tries to gain entrance to your mind - visualize the needle leaning toward the red - or negative side and know that the thought will cause you injury. Then you will at once reverse your thinking moving the needle back to the *happy*, prosperous side

POSITIVE THOUGHTS

LOVE
Friendship
Understanding
Tolerance
Health
Strength
Generosity
Youth
Respect
SUCCESS

NEGATIVE THOUGHTS

Hatred
Jealousy
Anger
Intolerance
Illness
Weakness
Selfishness
Age
Disrespect
FAILURE

CHAPTER SIX

Work Less—Accomplish More

WHAT IS THE greatest asset of a millionaire? "His millions, of course," you will say. But you will not be right. His greatest asset is *NOT* his money, *NOT* his estate, *NOT* his power in the community.

You might, by this time, arrive at the conclusion that, if his money is not his greatest asset, then the most valuable asset a millionaire can have is his ability to make the millions. And the correctness of his opinion depends upon your interpretation of the word *ABILITY*. If you interpret ability as education, knowledge of business and business laws, again you will be wrong.

A millionaire's greatest asset is his *SUCCESS CONSCIOUSNESS*, that state of mind whereby he *KNOWS* he will succeed.

Universities and colleges are graduating thousands and thousands of men and women yearly who are well equipped with the type of training which could make them successful in the world of business; yet, statistics reveal that a very small percentage reach great heights.

If you were to be given the opportunity of studying those who do reach the pinnacle of success, in comparison with those who just get by, what difference would you find? By now, you have progressed far enough with your study of *CREATIVE PSYCHOLOGY* to know the answer. A man succeeds if he *KNOWS* he can't fail, because, engraved in his mind is the radiance of the all powerful words: "I AM A SUCCESS!"

All right, I'm going to tell you that this very service can be rendered for you. Your *CREATIVE MIND* is the *MAGICAL MIND,* which is at your service twenty-four hours each day, and which will work on your problems for you while your *CONSCIOUS MIND* is otherwise engaged. Fantastic? To the contrary. If you are not now enjoying the best from life, it is undoubtedly due to the fact that you are not taking advantage of the service which your *CREATIVE MIND* is able and willing to render.

Therefore, from this chapter onward, I want you to be doubly thoughtful. *THINK* as you read. As the various thoughts are revealed to you, instead of merely *reading* them, think about them and how they apply to *your* life. You do not go to a store to buy a new garment without visualizing how you would look wearing it. I want you to do that same visualizing with these thoughts.

This chapter is unusually important, and from it you will gain a lot; not that *that,* which you will learn, is more powerful than the information I have already given to you; but you have now developed to a point where it *means more* to you than this same material would have meant prior to this time. And, so that you will get the most good from this, I have a suggestion to make: Make certain you are thoroughly comfortable and relaxed, then close your eyes for a few minutes and mentally review the previous chapters. As you do so, rejoice in the thought that you are reviewing the material which is forming the foundation of a richer, happier life. Doing this will put you in the frame of mind whereby you will obtain far more good from this work.

When the problems of life seem a bit trying, have you ever wished that you could close your eyes and go to sleep for a period of time, and that some magical mind would do the solving of your problems for you? Probably you have, as this sort of wishful thinking is common with most people.

Robert Updegraff said: "It is not so much a lack of Brain-Power or of business capacity or acumen that keeps men from progressing faster toward their objectives and toward a solid position in the world. It is, rather, because they take only half a mind into business with them. The result is that they work their conscious mind too hard, too many hours of the day, and too many days of the year. We feel virtuous, because we work so hard and so conscientiously that we are tired, whereas we should feel ashamed that we work so hard, and make so little progress, and we are weary of mind." Mr. Updegraff meant by "half a mind" that we attempt to do all of our work *consciously* without taking advantage of the tremendous reservoir of power at our command through the *CREATIVE MIND.*

In this chapter you will begin forming the habit of putting the *CREATIVE MIND* to work for you. This servant is on the job twenty-four hours every day and, as you learn to use that great force, that endless source of intelligence at your disposal, you will find that consciously you will have more time for recreation and enjoyment.

Have you ever observed that those people who accomplish the most are the ones who, quite apparently, work the least?

The President of the United States will actually take several vacation periods each year, and we all know the vast amount of work resting on the shoulders of the chief executive.

Heads of large institutions will, as a rule, take at least two vacations each year; yet we know the responsibilities they have. One prominent executive once made the statement that he could not do all of his work in twenve months of the year, yet he could in ten. Does this sound like a conundrum?

In an early chapter you learned that in each subsequent one there would be one big dominant thought. In this chapter the message which is revealed to you is: the *CREATIVE MIND does its best work while the CONSCIOUS MIND is either in abeyance or pleasantly occupied.*

This gives you the happy news that, to be successful, instead of working harder, and for more hours, it is really essential that you take more time for enjoyable diversion. This is made possible by utilizing the forces of the *CREATIVE MIND* to do your constructive creating and planning. Your *CONSCIOUS MIND* then puts into action the results from the work of your *CREATIVE MIND*.

Thomas Jay Hudson—in commenting on the powers of the *CREATIVE MIND,* which he refers to as the Subjective Mind, said: "The truth is, that all phenomena of the Subjective Mind go to prove that it is the most intensely Conscious Mind that we know anything of; that it is constantly alert, sleeplessly active, and untiringly vigilant. Its potentially perfect memory has been made manifest in thousands of ways. Its intuitive knowledge of the laws of its being is a matter of history. Its prodigious power of rapid mentation, as shown by mathematical prodigies, is well known to every investigator. That it is, in short, intensely conscious and infinitely more than can possibly be cognized by the objective senses, is the most certain and significant truth revealed by our modern experimental psychology."

Perhaps by now a big question is forming in your mind. "If I work my *CREATIVE MIND* twenty-four hours each day, won't I always be mentally tired?" My answer to this question is, that right now, your *CREATIVE MIND IS WORKING TWENTY-FOUR HOURS EACH DAY.* If it is not being directed into positive, constructive channels through constructive thinking, it will be working against you by following the *negative* thoughts.

In this chapter I wish to emphasize two very important points:

1. *Your CREATIVE MIND, if permitted to, will direct you in your work, making it better, easier to perform, and far more pleasant.*

2. *You can, at will, direct your CREATIVE MIND to assist you in the solving of problems; helping you in making the right decisions; creating ways and means of greater achievement.*

At this point, I will suggest that, before proceeding further, you lay this book aside for a while and think about the things you have already learned. If you have found yourself growing tense through the emotional excitement these thoughts might have stirred within you—*RELAX*. In the pages to follow, you will be given a routine, enabling you to begin to live according to these principles, and it is important that you approach them under the most ideal conditions.

You have already been told that you do not become good in your work until after your *CREATIVE MIND* takes over. Now you will learn how to direct your *CREATIVE MIND* to still further help *YOU*.

1. *KNOW* that the *CREATIVE MIND* is occupied every hour of the day, and that it is either working *FOR* or *AGAINST* you.

2. *KNOW* that in your case your *CREATIVE MIND* is working *FOR* you—because you will hold nothing but *POSITIVE, CONSTRUCTIVE* thoughts.

3. *BE SPECIFIC* in the instructions you give to your *CREATIVE MIND*. If it is *better health* you want, *KNOW* that your *CREATIVE MIND* is directing the glands and organs of your body, to bring on conditions of *better health*—and that thoughts will come into your consciousness, directing you to do the things necessary to promote *better health*. *If you desire further advancement* in your work, *KNOW* that your *CREATIVE MIND* will direct you to take the steps necessary to *assure* advancement. If problems

stand between you and your happiness, *KNOW* that your *CREATIVE MIND,* with its reasoning faculties, will provide a practical solution for you. In short, *KNOW* that your *CREATIVE MIND* stands ready, able and willing to assist you in any way you may desire.

4. *FREE YOUR MIND FROM WORRY.* You have learned that your *CREATIVE MIND* is the seat of intelligence, and if you have been thoughtful as you have read these pages, you will know that the maximum amount of intelligence which one might have *consciously,* is nothing at all compared to that which we all have—in our *CREATIVE MINDS.* Chapter Seven is devoted to worry and how to overcome it. What you will gain from it will make you happy indeed.

5. *HAVE FAITH.* Make certain that you are not merely *wishing* for better conditions through your *CREATIVE MIND;* but rather sense a feeling of *MASTERY,* which comes when you fully understand the truth of the statement made in an earlier chapter to the effect that the *CONSCIOUS MIND* is the *MASTER*—the *CREATIVE MIND* the *SERVANT.*

A woman once came to me for counsel regarding her problem. She had a husband with whom she could not get along. She received practically no money for clothes, and had no time to earn any money, because of the time required in caring for her two children. She felt that my teachings were for the other fellow, not for her. She was so badly off her case seemed hopeless, and, furthermore, she could not find time necessary to study for self-improvement.

I told her that the answer to all her problems was contained in her *CREATIVE MIND* and that, if she could have *FAITH* in the *CREATIVE MIND*, she could find happiness. I was not so sure that my talk of an hour or more had made an impression on her, so set was she in her own opinion.

Six months later, she came back to me and had changed so amazingly, I did not recognize her. She actually had difficulty in making me remember the sorrowful creature she had been previous to that time.

She had accepted the thought that her *CREATIVE MIND* held the answers to her problems. She had reached the state of consciousness where she *KNEW* that she would be guided to do all the things necessary to get along with her husband. She *KNEW* too she would receive the thoughts which would enable her to acquire a fine wardrobe. She *KNEW* the problems of rearing her children would *cease* to be problems.

This woman related, with great enthusiasm, that her married life was now ideal. She had plenty of fine garments in her wardrobe, and her children were now a joy instead of a care. And, with all of these blessings, her new found happiness had made her look—*and feel*—many years younger than when she first visited me.

If I had cited this case earlier, it would have seemed a bit too good to be true. But to you who have progressed this far, the results obtained by this woman are most normal indeed—and to be expected.

So far, I have given you the routine in contacting the source of power and intelligence in your *CREATIVE MIND*—for your daily good. There are times, however, when situations will arise, where special assistance is required. You might have to make a very important decision. You cannot afford to make a mistake—and you are at a loss to know which way to turn. It might be: changing your job, buying a piece of property, going into business, or any one of a thousand different things. All right, your faithful *CREATIVE MIND,* with its independent reasoning faculties, will help you with an answer.

Earlier you learned that the *CREATIVE MIND is alert* twenty-four hours of the day, and you also learned that it works best when the *CONSCIOUS MIND* is either pleasantly occupied or in abeyance. It would appear, therefore, that the best time to submit a problem to your *CREATIVE MIND* would be either before retiring at night or as you are entering a period of recreation.

I am going to give you a routine to follow when you are calling upon your *CREATIVE MIND* for special assistance. After you have followed it for a period of time—it will become so much a part of you you will follow it without any conscious mental effort. You will automatically use the procedure in placing a command with your *CREATIVE MIND* for action.

As you fully grasp the importance of this principle, you will understand what I meant when I told you of the executive who could not accomplish all of his work in twelve months—but could in ten. He would take the periods of relaxation and recreation, on his yacht or farm, to give his *CREATIVE MIND* the opportunity to work on the important tasks confronting him. You will also understand that in the future your own life will present a better balance between work and play.

All right, here is the regime to follow in connection with special help from your *CREATIVE MIND.*

1. *RELAX*—both mentally and physically. It is not a bad idea to frequently review Chapter Four on the *ART OF RELAXATION.* It is *IMPORTANT.*

2. *THINK OF YOUR PROBLEM.* Think through on it—but do *NOT FEAR IT.* If you were to give a job to another person, you'd have to explain what it was you wanted done. This is true with your *CREATIVE MIND.* You are about to give to it a special assignment, so it is necessary that you visualize just *what it is* you desire from your *CREATIVE MIND.* Do *NOT FEAR IT,* because you will be turning it over to an intelligence far greater than the intelligence of your *CONSCIOUS MIND.*

3. *GAIN A SUCCESS ATTITUDE* regarding your problem. You can gain a Success Attitude, if you have developed *FAITH* in your *CREATIVE MIND.* You will *know* that it is ready, able and willing to serve you—and *WILL* serve you.

4. *AFTER YOU HAVE GONE THIS FAR,* just remove all, and I mean *ALL,* thoughts of the problem from your *CONSCIOUS MIND—KNOWING* that the solution will be forthcoming at the proper time.

Let us say, for example, you will have an important appointment at ten o'clock tomorrow morning, at which time you must make a momentous decision. You are calling upon your *CREATIVE MIND* this evening to help you to make the *right* decision. All right, after you have progressed through the routine, merely turn it over to your *CREATIVE MIND—KNOWING* that before ten o'clock tomorrow you *WILL HAVE THE ANSWER.*

You'll be amazed to find what is going to happen. Tomorrow morning you will awaken and find thoughts coming into your consciousness as to what you should do—and with this knowledge *will be the reasons*—why you should take such a step. The unfoldment will be so logical you will not be able to doubt it at all.

EXERCISES

Between now and the time you take up the study of the next chapter, begin gaining experience in making your CREATIVE MIND work FOR you. List all of those conditions you have looked at as worries, and one by one, step by step, seek a solution from the CREATIVE MIND.

WE THINK IN PICTURES

If I should mention the word "house" what would you see with your mind's eye? Would you see the letters h-o-u-s-e? No, you would see the picture of a house. You might see your own house, the house of a friend, or it might be the home of your dreams. In any event, you would see a house of some sort, and not the letters comprising the word. This is because the mind does not think in terms of words—but pictures. Everything we see, hear or read, we translate into mental pictures. In other words, we "see" what we hear and read.

In a previous chapter you learned that the *CREATIVE MIND* is influenced by the thoughts of the *CONSCIOUS MIND*. If we hold negative thoughts, we will get a negative reaction; if we hold positive thoughts, we will get a positive reaction. Keep this in mind, because it is so important, as you will realize as you continue. Your mental pictures are really patterns used by your *CREATIVE MIND*, just as a builder might use a blue-print.

There are two kinds of sight: *physical sight* and *mental sight*. Our *physical sight* brings to us the impressions we gain through our physical eyes. Our *mental sight* brings to us the impression—*mental picture—we gain through our "mind's eye"*.

Perhaps but a few people have realized this, but we see far more through our *mental sight* than we do through our *physical sight*. Here is a truth which perhaps has never occurred to you: Not a single ray of light ever reaches the brain. All light is stopped at the retina inside the eye—and goes no farther. The *impression* of light is carried to the brain.

The extent of your *seeing* does not stop with the objects before your gaze. For example: You focus your vision on some object—or group of objects. A picture of those objects, through your physical eyes, is projected to your brain—but this picture does not remain static. Your mind's eye continues to see, by constructing images or pictures, of other phases of the objects being viewed. For instance, you might be looking at a house through your physical eyes, and your mind's eye might supplement that picture by creating pictures of what could be inside of that house. That is what we call *imagination,* which, as it is defined by

Webster, means: *"Formation of mental images or objects not present to the senses."*

When you read, your physical eyes are following the printed words, but your mind's eye is creating pictures of the persons, or objects represented by those words. No two people will see the same mental pictures, even though they may be reading the same material. The type of pictures you create depends upon your general type of thinking.

If you have a positive, constructive, happy mind, the mental pictures you create will be of a positive nature. If, however, you have a negative, pessimistic, gloomy mind, the mental pictures will be of a negative nature.

The mind is never free from pictures, either those which we see through our physical eyes, or those created through the imagination.

In Chapter Five you learned that thoughts maintained in your *CONSCIOUS MIND* are accepted as instructions by your *CREATIVE MIND*—which acts accordingly.

In this chapter you are learning that you *think in terms of pictures*—not words. This will enable you to understand that your mental pictures are *PATTERNS,* which are acted upon by your *CREATIVE MIND.*

The dominant thought being developed now is: *You are AS you are—due to the type of thoughts you have been thinking up to this point. What you will be in weeks, months and years to come WILL DEPEND ON THE THOUGHTS you will hold FROM THIS POINT ON-WARD.* This last sentence will be encouraging to you, because it means that, if you are not satisfied with yourself as you are at this moment, you have *within your being the POWER* to change yourself—or any given situation—*by changing your THOUGHTS;* or as you now understand it, *creating new mental PICTURE-PATTERNS.*

In an earlier chapter you were asked to hold to the thought: *"I'm Filled With Power!"* If you did so, you experienced a sense of well-being each time you expressed the thought. Now, until you begin with the next chapter, I want you to repeat the following small sentences several times daily:

> "I CAN be a Success!"
> "I WILL be a Success!"
> "I AM a Success!"

When you first wake up in the morning, repeat these sentences several times. During the day, each time you think of it, do so. Before you retire at night, go through the routine again. These three sentences cover the three phases already outlined: The thought: "I CAN be a Success" is the phase of *RECOGNITION.* You recognize that you *CAN be a Success.*

"I WILL be a Success" represents the phase of *REALIZATION.* You *realize* that right thinking will bring you success—and since you have determined to think rightly, you *know you will be a Success.*

"I AM a Success" represents the third phase of *MANIFESTATION.* We first think in terms of success before we manifest success. This being true, we are a success the moment we gain *CONSCIOUSNESS of SUCCESS,* because we *KNOW* success is ours. Therefore, *knowing* that you *CAN* and *WILL be a success,* means that you *ARE* a success, because *SUCCESS WILL MANIFEST ITSELF TO YOU.*

CHAPTER SEVEN

How to Overcome Worry

WORRY, YOUR NUMBER ONE ENEMY OF SUCCESS, HEALTH AND HAPPINESS

IF YOU ARE not happy, it is safe to predict that you spend much time in worry. Everyone tells you that you should not worry, that it will not help the least bit. You agree with all of this, yet you ask the question: "How can I keep from worrying?"

Understanding just what worry really is will help you materially in overcoming it. You have learned that your thoughts are pictures. Worry is maintaining mental pictures of things *YOU DO NOT WANT*, instead of picturing things you *DO WANT*. To prove that this is true, merely analyze *WORRY* for a moment and you'll agree. For example: If you have a pain or an ache, what do you visualize? Do you see pictures of yourself as being radiantly healthy? NO! You are more likely to see pictures of your-self as being ill—and perhaps getting worse. You might carry the pictures on to a point of visualizing yourself going to the hospital, then the hospital and doctor bills etc., etc., etc. Isn't this true?

When you worry about your job, what kind of mental pictures do you see? Do you visualize yourself getting a promotion with a larger pay? Not very likely. You see yourself being dismissed, and then, perhaps, you carry on your mental pictures, seeing difficulties in getting another job. Right? Again you created pictures of *CONDITIONS YOU DO NOT WANT*.

When you worry about your business, what kind of pictures do you see? Do you see yourself going to the bank—carrying large moneybags filled with money resulting from increased business? Certainly not. You see business getting worse and perhaps failing completely. Pictures of *CONDI-TIONS YOU DO NOT WANT*.

"FOR THE THING WHICH I GREATLY FEARED HAS COME UPON ME." (Job 3.25) This verse is no doubt responsible for the proverb: "FEAR ATTRACTS THAT WHICH IS FEARED." Have you ever used the expression: "I was afraid of that"? You probably have; it is a common expression, especially after something has gone wrong. Is it just a coincidence when you fear something and it happens? Students of *CREATIVE PSYCHOL-OGY KNOW* that fear and worry actually set the laws of nature in motion to bring about that which has been feared.

So that this will not appear as bordering on some hokus-pokus ism, let me explain *WHY* fear attracts that which is feared.

First let me make one thing very clear. Nature does not bring on bad things as a punishment. You, yourself attract them to you. . . . If you hold the negative mental picture-patterns in your mind, nature doesn't ask you if you are suie this is what you want. Your picture-pattern automatically puts the forces to work in making a reality of the *CONDITION PICTURED*. If, in dialing a number on your telephone, you happen to make a mistake and dial the wrong number, the head of the telephone company does not give you a wrong person just to punish you. No, you dialed a wrong number, and in doing so, put the complicated mechanism at the telephone office into operation —and the telephone corresponding to the *wrong number* was called. If you hold a *negative mental picture,* you merely put the forces of nature to work in reproducing *THAT PICTURE* in your being or in your affairs. In other words, *you mentally dialed a wrong picture*—and you got a wrong result.

In Chapter Three, when you were asked to make out your lists of objectives, you were told to keep the lists available and to go over them at least twice daily. Now you will understand that, by doing so, you are training yourself to think in terms of things you *WANT,* instead of things you *DO NOT WANT.* But this is only one reason why you should refer to your lists of objectives frequently.

Your *CREATIVE MIND* is not necessarily confined within your body. It is *IN* and *AROUND* your body. It can project itself across the city, state, or even the country and the world, just as easy as it can project itself across the room. Since the *CREATIVE MIND* has reasoning faculties independent of the *CONSCIOUS MIND,* it can *readily be seen that, by visualizing any desired condition with FAITH, IT WILL COME TO PASS.* Your *CREATIVE MIND* can reason ways and means to bring it about

—and even project itself to points necessary to aid in the manifestation.

Therefore: The way to get what you want is *to visualize yourself as having and* MAKING USE *of the particular objective*. Don't think of it with a wishing attitude. Wishing is negative. It indicates that you do not have that for which you are wishing—and furthermore you do not *EXPECT* to get it—otherwise you would not find it necessary to wish.

Return again to your list of objectives. Now, instead of merely reading words written on paper, see yourself *ACTUALLY POSSESSING EACH AND EVERY ONE* of them. If an objective is physical, see yourself enjoying *RADIANT HEALTH*. With your material objectives, see yourself *USING* and *ENJOYING* these objectives.

You might wonder just *HOW* these objectives will come into being. It is interesting to observe the operation of natural laws in this regard. You will find yourself being led—as if by an invisible hand—to do the things necessary to realize your objectives.

One student who took my college course wrote: "It is now practically a year since I took your course—and just last night I was looking over my list of objectives, which I wrote down when I first enrolled. To my astonishment every one had become real—except *one*—and *that* is almost materialized. Many of the objectives, when I first put them on paper, seemed so impossible I had difficulty in getting the courage to include them."

A young lady came to me and said that my theories were beautiful, but that they do not work. She said she had wished for things all her life, yet she never got anything but just the necessities. She did not realize that she revealed the reason for her failure in just one little word she used: "wished". She said she had wished for things. I told her that she would never have anything but the wishes until she could reach that state of consciousness whereby she would *KNOW* those objectives were meant for her. Her face colored a bit as she admitted I must be right. She said: "As I think about it, I have always *known* that I would have this and that trouble—and I was never disappointed; the troubles invariably showed up. Hereafter I will *know* I will be a success." Within a year this little lady was bragging to all her friends that *now* she *knows HOW* to get anything she wants. And she *IS* getting things she only dreamed of before.

*   *   *

Later you will learn how your thoughts affect those around you—how you influence and are influenced by thought. You will gain further understanding regarding the laws of attraction and how our thoughts attract to us those things which are visioned—whether they are good or bad.

You pass through three phases in attaining the state where you reach the pinnacle of happiness and success.

The first phase is that of *RECOGNITION*. You recognize that thoughts are things, and that thoughts you think have a definite bearing on the type of life you live. Your interest carries you on through further investigation, until you reach . . .

The second phase, which is that of *REALIZATION*. You realize that you are *as you are*, because of the thoughts you have been thinking and that, to change your future, you must change your thoughts. You change your attitude toward life and things from the *wishing state,* to that of *KNOWING.* In other words, that state of mind where you *KNOW, BEYOND GUESSING, HOPING* or *TRYING* that *SUCCESS, BETTER HEALTH* and *HAPPINESS* are your rightful heritage—and that they *ARE YOURS.* This brings you to . . .

The third and final phase, which is *MANIFESTATION.* At this *point you know that you really are MASTER OF YOUR FATE AND CAPTAIN OF YOUR SOUL.*

One day, after a broadcast, I received a telephone call from a man, asking me if I would join him for dinner, that he had a success story to tell me which I might like to incorporate in one of my broadcasts. His story would be an inspiration to anyone.

Through circumstances, this man was forced to take over a small manufacturing business, which was so badly in debt it looked like the sheriff's notice would soon be posted on the door. It seemed like a case where only a miracle would save the business. This man was in poor health and had had very little experience in that particular business.

Just about the time this dark picture was getting darker and more hopeless, this man had an awakening. He had begun a study of *CREATIVE PSYCHOLOGY* and had already entered the phase of *RECOGNITION*—and was about to enter that of *REALIZATION.* One day he asked himself why he had not made use of his *CREATIVE MIND* in helping him to put over this business. He decided then and there to do so. He followed very much the same pattern as was given to you in Chapter Six. From that time on, things began to happen. He was not only able to wipe off all indebtedness, but had purchased and paid for over $100,000 worth of additional machinery. His enthusiastic words to me were: "Ben, I'll never want for anything again. I now have the key to abundant supply." In addition to the success he had made, his health had improved quite materially.

I have laid out seven simple steps to use in overcoming worry. They will prove most effective if you will carefully follow them.

STEP ONE. Worry is static. It creates a mental condition which could be vividly described by saying it resembles a form of mental paralysis, where the mind stands still and the inner eye gazes in a fashion of horror at mental pictures of gloom, dismay, and even disaster.

Step One is to *know* that to permit worry to enter the mind is to sanction a condition which blocks all progress and deprives one of happiness.

STEP TWO. "How can I stop worrying?" one might ask. This and similar questions have been asked by nearly everyone who worries—and this covers much ground, because most people worry. Whenever I am confronted with this question, I counter with another: "Has worry ever helped you in any way?" The answer is, of course, "no".

At this point to offer the admonition "Don't worry!" would not be good advice, or, I might say, incomplete advice. To merely ask a worrier to stop worrying would imply that he should nonchalantly toss the problem over his shoulder and do nothing about it.

If worry is focused on a disturbing problem, to merely suggest that one forget it, would probably prove more disastrous than worry. Worry, at least, indicates cognizance of the existence of a problem. What must be done, therefore, is to find a *constructive* substitute for the worry—something which will solve the problem instead of permitting it to remain as a mental bugaboo.

STEP THREE. We have already learned that worry means the holding of mental pictures of *things you do not want*. We can add to this statement by saying that mental pictures representing the object of the worry, really supply the Creative Mind with negative, destructive patterns, which not only disturb the peace of mind, but which actually put the forces of nature to work toward bringing the negative conditions into being. Therefore, this step is to *know* that worry cannot help in any way, but will tend toward making a reality of that which prompted the worry.

A man was just starting a new job and did so with fear. In the past, soon after getting started on a new job, he would lose it. He worried for fear the same thing would happen with the newest job. He was told to concentrate on doing a good job instead of worrying as to whether or not he would hold it. He followed the suggestion and not only held the job but gained several promotions.

STEP FOUR. There is a solution to every problem, otherwise it would not be a problem. If you will know this to be true and that you have the means at your command of finding the solution, you will have just cause for gladness instead of worry.

When one worries it indicates his lack of faith in his own ability to overcome the disturbing problem.

If you accept a problem as a challenge instead of a cause for worry, an entirely new spirit will come to the fore. Just as worry tears one down, the victory over a disturbing situation will provide a stimulating satisfaction.

STEP FIVE. "Worry prevents one from doing the very thing which would provide the means to prevent the worry."

The story is told of a man who sought advice after having spent a day and night of constant worry. "Approximately how many hours have you spent worrying about this matter?" he was asked. After a few moments of reflection, he estimated about ten hours, counting the time he had spent during the day and also the hours after retiring. "Today," advised the psychologist, "spend just five hours, according to the clock, in constructive thinking as to ways and means of solving the problem." In exactly three hours a logical, constructive plan was evolved; less than one-third of the time he had previously spent in worry.

This step, therefore, is to discipline yourself to take a constructive view toward those situations which might have been disturbing you. In the final analysis, about the only difference between worry and progress is a matter of attitude. The one with a constructive mind will take all conditions in stride and consider them merely as steps on the pathway of life.

A college graduate inherited a business which was about to go into bankruptcy. It was heavily in debt; had but little business, and needed much new, modern equipment.

Instead of appearing as a monumental worry to this energetic young man, he took an interesting viewpoint regarding the problem confronting him.

"Suppose this were a problem presented to me in college in connection with my studies—how would I solve it?" he asked himself. This provocative query could not go unanswered. He, therefore, approached the problem in the spirit that there was an answer—and he found it.

STEP SIX. Have you ever watched the sun breaking through a heavy blanket of clouds? The once drab earth seems to take on a radiance which immediately dispels all semblance of dreariness. The grass appears greener. There's an exciting brilliance to the song of the birds. And your own problems quickly assume an air of less importance.

There are mental clouds which we allow to fog our own thinking and reasoning, and which can be dispersed with a ray of sunshine in the form of thoughts of happiness.

If, at the time of viewing disturbing problems, you can find reason to be happy, you will have far greater ease in developing a solution. In fact, you will actually enjoy working on the problem which might otherwise give you hours of mental torment.

This step, then, will be to approach your problems with a happy mind. Yes, you can have a happy mind—even in face of elements which could normally be disturbing. For one thing, you can be happy in the thought that you are *master of your being* and that you are bigger than the problems confronting you. This step is of far greater importance than may seem on the surface.

STEP SEVEN. In the previous chapter you learned

how to use your Creative Mind in making decisions for you and helping you to solve your problems. After having followed through the six steps so far given, then, as your seventh step, turn the problem over to your Creative Mind *knowing* you will get the most practical solution.

It will not always be necessary to review these steps in connection with worries which might come to you. After you have followed this routine on a few specific cases, it will become natural for you to follow the suggested formula without realizing it. It will become almost automatic.

CHAPTER EIGHT

The Value of Self-Appreciation

A YOUNG SALESMAN, about to "throw in the sponge," was brought to me by his wife who hoped I could help him make a success of the work he was in.

He was a clean-cut lad, had a good education, spoke very well; yet, he was not ringing the bell so far as orders were concerned. Discouraged, he was about to give up selling and take some sort of a routine job which would pay a fixed but certain salary.

The plucky wife of this unhappy man had faith that if he could once make a start, he could roll up the type of income so many other salesmen are making.

I talked with this fellow for quite a while, and at length came to a definite conclusion. There was only one basic fault with this would-be salesman: he had no faith in himself. There was no self-appreciation! He saw himself as a failure, and tried to prove it to me by showing how few orders he would get in the course of a day.

A five-word formula was given this man, and it raised him from a position where he was barely making a living to the top position in his organization.

What is this five-word formula? You will probably laugh at it just as our salesman friend did. In fact, I had to "talk like a Dutch Uncle" in order to persuade him to even try it. Yet, after one understands the psychology underlying the formula, it is quite easy to see how it could be so effective.

"You are what you think you are," was the essence of what I told this chap. He was a poor salesman because he could not see himself as anything else. Daily he would go through the motions of selling, but inwardly did not really expect to make any sales. Occasionally he would encounter someone who was looking for that which he had to sell and he would get the order; but it was not salesmanship which landed it; an office boy could have done as much.

I made my visitor promise that for a solid week, many times each day, he would repeat to himself: "I Am a Great Salesman." There was disappointment on his face, and his eager-eyed, loyal wife, who sat nearby, had difficulty in suppressing her feelings. They had expected me to lay out a long, complicated routine to be followed, instead of giving what appeared to be a fantastic remnant from the days of superstition.

He kept his promise! When he returned to me a week later for a checkup, he was a different man. A look of determination had replaced the air of defeat he originally carried. Then he told me that already his sales were mounting and it was not long before he began to climb over the heads of many who had been with the company far more years than he had.

To you who have read this far in this book, it will be readily understood why this simple formula produced such outstanding results. There is nothing magical about the formula. The thought: "I am a great salesman," is accepted by the Creative Mind as an instruction. It proceeds to act on this fact with the result that a new spirit is born. Thoughts of success begin flowing through the mind and soon the one so activated will begin thinking in terms of arguments which will gain orders, rather than ways of gracefully accepting defeat.

A lecturer who travels the country over, admitted that before every talk he gives he says to himself: "This will be the best talk I have ever given." People who have heard him several times are invariably remarking that he seems to constantly be getting better. And he is getting better! He is using sound psychological principles in getting the maximum amount of help from his Creative Mind.

In talking about self-appreciation before audiences, I have often been asked if it isn't egotistical for one to develop self-appreciation. Of course, the answer is "no". I wouldn't like to trust the life of a loved one in the hands of a surgeon who did not believe in himself, would you? Or, would you like to trust an important legal matter with a lawyer who did not believe in himself? I am sure you understand what I am referring to.

Many people have deplored the fact they did not have any talent. Some will wish they could paint; others might have a desire to write; then you'll find those with a preference for music who will pity themselves because they are not musical. Do you know that the desire for an accomplishment is Nature's way of telling us that we have the necessary talent to bring it into being? Many, many experiments have been conducted proving this to be so.

A certain wife had always wished she could become an artist, but was sure she could not, since, as she said, she could not draw a straight line. Her husband, as a psychological experiment, bought a complete outfit of colors, canvasses, brushes, easel, etc., and presented it to her for Christmas. In giving them to her he said he would enjoy seeing her try her hand at painting, because she had such a marvelous sense of color. He commented on her intuitive knowledge of color harmony; that she had an uncommon feeling for balance, as indicated by the manner in which she arranged furnishings in her home. What this husband did was to give his wife an *awareness* of the existence of a talent. This little lady "tried her hand" at painting and even amazed herself by the facility with which she handled her brushes and colors. Now her home is alive with paintings which arrest the attention and admiration of all who see them.

There is a young lady who has become a really good pianist because she was told that she had talent for music, notwithstanding the fact she had always felt otherwise. The experimenter said he could detect musical talent due to her natural rhythm and ability to carry a tune while humming or singing. A piano was purchased and in a remarkably short time she was doing a genuinely good job in playing it. You see? She had gained an *awareness* of a talent for music.

Many years ago, a young man wanted to raise a few dollars, and to do so, attempted to sell a phonograph and a collection of records he possessed. He wrote a letter to an acquaintance who, he felt, might be induced to make such a purchase. The man not only bought the outfit but in answering the letter he received, commented on it in a highly complimentary way. "You'd make a mighty good advertising man," this writer said, "because you have the faculty of expressing your thoughts in such an appealing manner." Up to that time the seller of the phonograph had never given a thought to the field of advertising. But, what happened? He entered this fascinating occupation and did not stop until he was head of a large and conspicuously prosperous advertising agency in New York City. That man became a success in the field of advertising after he had gained an *awareness* that he had talent in that direction.

This chapter relates to appreciation of self. Self-appreciation is another way of referring to *awareness* of that which one might possess.

An outstanding orator tells of the day he first became *aware* of his talent as a speaker. At a meeting of a small club of which he was a member, he was called upon to give a report regarding his committee. As he took his seat, the president of the club asked him, "Have you ever given any thought to public speaking?" The member blushingly shook his head in the negative. The president suggested that he should do so, telling him that he had platform poise, an interesting delivery, a good choice of words, etc. From that moment onward, this man started to see himself as a public speaker; he became cognizant of the fact that he could speak—and it was not long before his awareness that *self-appreciation* became manifest and he quickly developed into a speaker of note.

"How can *I* acquire self-appreciation?" you might ask. "How can I become *aware* of talents I might have?" And,

...tions it would make me happy
... we seldom ask questions on subjects of little
or no interest to us. And, even asking the questions indicates an awareness that you *can* do things, otherwise you
would not care to know *how* to do them.

There are five simple steps one may follow in acquiring self-appreciation:

1. *Know what you want.* Frequently we hear one express the thought that he does not know what he wants.
Perhaps he does not realize it, but such a statement is not
true. It usually means that he has no faith in his ability
to acquire anything worthwhile, and, of those things which
he thinks he can get, he knows nothing of sufficient value
to prove of interest to him.

Using the same words as were given in an early portion
of this book, let me ask: "If you could have anything you
wanted, what would you want?" Right now I am not referring to *things* as much as to *talents*—because with the
talents we get the things.

Step One, therefore, is to know what it is you would
like to do, or be.

2. *The desire indicates you have the talent.* Recall the
illustrations already given in this chapter. If your desire
is to write, *know* that you have the talent which will enable you to become a successful writer. If you long for a
business of your own, know you have the talent which
can be directed toward the attainment of your objective.

It is hard for one to believe that a desire indicates the
existence of a talent, and here is why: We do not take into
consideration that it will require a bit of time to gain the

experience which will be necessary in connection with the desire.

To assume that by having a desire to do a certain thing—play a musical instrument for example—that one could at once sit down and play the moment he became aware that he had musical talent, would be foolish, of course. The desire means that you *can* be successful in music—and you *will be* if you back your desire with action.

This thought may prove a bit discouraging to a certain type of individual. He could easily feel that here the reason is being revealed why so few people get what they want—too much work is required in bringing the desire into manifestation. However, if you have been thoughtful while reading this far, this thought will not occur to you. You will know that by putting your Creative Mind to work with and for you in connection with your desire, you will have a parade of thrills, as you see a continuity of things happening during the time your objective comes nearer and nearer.

3. *You are a mind with a body.* This is no longer news to you, and you will find it referred to again before you reach the last pages of the book.

One reason why it may be difficult to quickly accept that which is being given in this chapter is because you have never *seen* yourself doing the things you might desire to do.

That body of yours is just a utility for your mind, ready and willing to follow instructions at all times. And, right here, you may be set to take issue with me. You might agree with me up to a certain point, then you'll point out that one must have a normal body which is in good condition. I'll concede that it would do a one-legged man very little good to aspire to be a foot-racer; or a one-armed man to become a boxer; but, even people so handicapped can climb to great heights—if their objectives are within the realm of possibilities.

I knew a man whose body was largely paralyzed. His limbs were motionless. There was no movement at all in one of his arms; he could use the other arm slightly. He knew he was a mind with a body and that there were no limitations to his thinking. His body was a utility to his mind, but as it was, it could not function to any great extent.

Before going further, let us realize that each member of the body is, in reality, an extension of mind. Our hands assist in carrying out thoughts through writing, working, assisting in eating, etc. Our legs and feet provide locomotion. The eyes, nose, mouth, ears, etc., are all extensions of mind, each intended to perform certain functions.

Through mind we can *create* further extensions of mind. We cannot drive nails with our hands, so we conceived the hammer which will enable us to do so. The hammer, therefore, is an extension of mind.

As the boundaries of civilization expanded, it was found that the legs alone were insufficient to furnish adequate locomotion to enable us to cover all of the newly explored and developed countries. Wagons, trains, automobiles, and airplanes were created—which, in reality, are extensions of mind.

Referring again to the paralyzed man, he found that his

present physical utilities were not functioning sufficiently well to keep up with his mental and visual requirements, so he proceeded to provide himself with further mental extensions. He designed a bed which embodied a desk. There was a telephone, writing pads, pencils, etc., all placed within easy access of his usable arm. There were gadgets galore—all acting as extensions of the mind. An inter-communication system was in operation between his bed-desk and the front door. Should the door-bell ring, he could talk to the one on the outside, and if he wished to admit the caller, the press of a button unlocked and opened the door.

So long as the mind is functioning, there are no physical limitations, provided the mind is positive in its thinking. As we think about these phases of being, it is easy to conclude that man's greatest handicap is a negative mind.

4. *It is easier to get what you want than to pity yourself for not having it.*   When just a young man I lived next door to one who was far more successful than I had been. He was earning, as a department manager, $42 per week. My salary was $25 per week. This, of course, was during the time when these figures represented the average earnings. I was intensely envious of this neighbor. Every time he would pass my house I would think of the number of things he could do with his income which I couldn't do with mine. I didn't seriously consider ways and means of bolstering my own income; I felt it would take too long —and too much work—to reach his station in life. As I now look back over my previous situation, I understand how much more difficult it was for me to stand still merely feeling sorry for myself, when I could have been enjoying the

thrill of accomplishment, had I taken that "envying time" and directed it into constructive channels.

Step Four is to know that the only difficult thing about self-improvement is the effort it takes to get started. Once you make the initial move—no matter how insignificant it might appear, all thoughts of effort—both mental and physical—will disappear as you see yourself moving on the road to achievement.

5. *Make your initial start now.* I suggest that the moment you finish reading this chapter, you lay your book aside and reflect for a moment on what this last chapter has meant to you. You are inspired right now—I know you are. You are, perhaps for the first time, beginning to see a new life of great accomplishment opening before you.

You decide you are *going* to do something about it. You are *going* to make your life a success. You are *going* to be ideally happy.

That word "going" will defeat you, if you permit it to. "Going" means motion, which ordinarily is good, but when the word is used in connection with intentions, it means that they are *going* and will always be ahead of you. You never quite catch up with them.

You have seen the dog with a stick under his collar and on the end of the stick will be tied a bone. The dog runs after the bone but never reaches it because it always remains static—the same distance from his mouth.

Your intentions might be perfectly good when you say you are *going* to do certain things. That word is the soul of indefiniteness. It could mean a week, month, year or many years—and too frequently goes on into infinity which to us means never.

My object in suggesting you lay this book aside after reading this chapter is to enable you to change the word *going* to *now*.

Before continuing your reading, take a step toward your objective. That step need not be a big one; something so that you can look yourself in the face and know you have started.

A young man once told me he could not save money—and bemoaned the fact that he could not do things he would do if he had money. I picked up a cardboard box and sealed the cover with Scotch tape, then proceeded to cut a slot in the top of it. I labeled the box: "Saving Fund." Then I asked him for a coin of any denomination. He handed me a five-cent piece. I dropped it through the slot, handed the box back to him and showed him that he had started saving. With that diminutive start, he formed a new habit, later built a home for himself and is climbing rapidly.

Your last step is to *start*. If you do nothing more than make a telephone call, or write a letter asking for inform tion—do it now! You will have started.

Remember, no looking in the next chapter until you do what is urged in this one.

CHAPTER NINE

How to Gain Self-Mastery!

'KNOW THYSELF," are perhaps the two most quoted words in our language. Authors and lecturers will refer to the philosopher of old—and in quoting those historical words will offer it as good advice, concluding that everyone should know himself.

To merely know yourself can be negative as well as helpful. To know yourself means to know your strong points *and* your weak ones. Most people—when learning about themselves will take everything for granted and resign themselves to the thought that, "I am as I am and there is little I can do about it."

It is not strange to hear people refer to themselves by saying, "I am mechanical," or "I am not mechanical." Regarding music, you will find some saying, "I am musical," while others will say, "I am not musical," etc. As to the psychological conditions, some will say, "I am timid," while others will declare their freedom from timidity.

It *is* advisable to "know thyself." A fault cannot be corrected until it is observed—but to merely know yourself is not enough. You must go a step further. You must *"master thyself."*

Perhaps at this point it might be well to refer back to the statement earlier made to the effect that human beings are *minds* with bodies, not bodies with minds. When we think of our bodies as utilities for the mind, we can gain a new concept of self-mastery. There can be no doubt but that the mind is master over the body (or should be)—so, then, self-mastery merely becomes a matter of exercising the rights vested in the mind.

You step into your automobile and feel you have complete mastery over the car. The motor starts when you take the proper steps. The car will move forward or backward; to the right or left—just as you will it to do. After it has provided transportation for you according to your wishes, you can put it away, stop the motor, and it remains motionless until you again elect to put it to work for you.

Exercising your self-mastery means guiding the body to do as you direct it. When your body dictates to the mind that you cannot do this or that, or that you must do certain things, then you are not master of yourself.

The individual who is master of his being might not be musical—but it is not because he can't be. It is because he has not taken any interest in music. Perhaps he has done little or no creative writing. This, too, is merely because up to the present, his desires have not pointed in that direction. He may not have shown any artistic tendencies, but that, again, merely signified there has been no inclination to delve into art. In short, the one with self-mastery never thinks in terms of "I can't do this or that." He *knows* he can, should he wish to do so.

"Is there any way of telling what talent I have?" I am often asked. Yes, there is a way. Nature will tell you if you listen. Have you ever realized that Nature tells you most of the things you should know? When the body needs nourishment, you become hungry. When the body needs moisture, you become thirsty. When the body needs rest for the restoration of worn tissue, you become tired. When you have a strong desire to do any particular thing, that is Nature telling you that you can do it if you want to.

You might love music, yet there is no instrument you can play. You sit down to the piano and can play nothing which sounds like music. This may give you cause to take issue with what I have been saying. But, I will repeat that because of your liking for music—and your desire to play—there is an indication that you *can* play. Perhaps it may be well to again emphasize that you must distinguish between wishing and knowing. Wishing that you could play is no evidence of self-mastery—just the opposite, in fact. To wish for anything is an evidence that you don't have it, nor do you expect to have it, otherwise you would not wish for it. The master, should he wish to take up music, will say to himself, in effect: "I like music and will take up an instrument" (mentioning whether piano, organ, violin, etc.), "because I know I will be able to play it shortly."

If the master's desires should run along commercial lines, he might think: "I'm tired of working for others, I'm going into business for myself, and I will succeed. I have an alert mind and it will quickly grasp the knowledge I must have in order to be successful."

During the question period in one of my classes, a student asked the question: "Suppose you wanted to do something and you just knew you couldn't do it, what then?"

"Be specific," I insisted, "just what was it you wanted to do?"

"I want to be a writer, but I know I never could write," she answered.

"Who told you you couldn't write?" I queried.

"No one. But I haven't any talent in that direction," she added.

"Have you ever tried to write?" I asked, politely facetious.

"What's the use?" she replied listlessly.

For a solid half-hour, I talked to this girl (and for the benefit of all other students) showing her that she could write if she really wanted to.

Within six months from that eventful evening, she had had a story accepted and was definitely on her way toward being an outstanding writer.

Without her realizing it, she had actually been resisting the impulse to write. She *wanted* to write but insisted she could not do so.

It must be explained that merely telling this student she could write and ordering her to do so, would not help a bit. In fact, it would probably help her to prove that she was right when she proclaimed she could not write.

It may be interesting to note here that when this lady did reach the state of consciousness where she *knew* she could write, her use of the English language was not the best—and her vocabulary was not too large.

The fact that she became aware she could write caused her to eagerly study words, their use and meaning. Her manner of expression grew more picturesque. A seed planted will attract from the earth and atmosphere the elements necessary to enable it to successfully bring a plant or tree into being. A seed-thought planted in our Creative Mind will guide us to take the steps necessary to make an actuality of that originally pictured in the mind.

The little lady earlier referred to reached a state of consciousness whereby she *knew* she could write. That seed-thought guided her to do the things which would enable her to reach her goal.

A young man worried over his future. He worked in a factory in a routine sort of a job, and was making no progress. His principle handicap was timidity. He had no friends because he did not try to make any. His income was small and he was just getting by—living a hand-to-mouth existence.

Conversing with this fellow brought to light he had inventive ability—but was doing nothing about it. Referring to a statement in Chapter Three: "You are what you think you are!" we have a splendid example in the case of this timid soul.

He saw himself as a timid individual—so tightly placed in a groove—he never would make any showing for himself.

Some gain a new consciousness faster than others—and this proved to be true with this man. After he had gained a new appreciation of himself and actually *saw* himself making full use of his inventive genius, he began to climb —and rapidly.

Many things happened to and for this man. Before the great transformation, he looked the part of a timid ne'er-do-well. There was a listless look in his eyes; he had a whine in his voice, a lag in his step. In other words, he reflected the impression he had of himself.

Today you would never associate the man you see now with the one formerly so discouraged. He stands erectly; has a determined set to his jaw; a friendly gleam in his eye. His voice is that of a man of affairs, one who knows exactly where he is going. And where is this man going? He is the president of a modest sized manufacturing plant.

Gaining self-mastery is comparatively simple; exceptionally so if you will thoughtfully follow the few simple steps I'll outine:

STEP ONE. The very first step one must take in gaining self-mastery is to have respect for himself. No man who has lost his self-respect can ever expect to be master of himself.

It is tragic when we realize how many people are being held back through a loss of self-respect. These individuals, either consciously or otherwise, feel they are not entitled to the good breaks of life, and they act accordingly. They might make feeble attempts to succeed and each time they fail, feel certain they were not meant to be happy or successful.

If you were called upon to forgive another for any wrong which had been done toward you, you would be happy to forgive, wouldn't you? You would forgive as cheerfully as you would look for forgiveness from others.

There is one person we never think of in connection with forgiveness—and that person is ourselves. At first it may seem strange to suggest that you forgive yourself, but as you think of it you realize that your body is just as much a part of humanity as the body of another; and if it is right to forgive another, it is equally right to forgive yourself. So, Step One, acquiring Self-Mastery, is to cleanse your heart and soul of all semblance of ill will which you might have been holding against yourself. Know that it is human to err, that everyone has erred at some time and instead of being held back by your mistakes of the past, you will profit by them.

To give you an idea of the importance of this first step, I will quote from a letter received from one who knows:

"Your remarks regarding self-forgiveness came to me as a blessing from heaven. In my younger days I guess I did almost everything bad except to kill. I have stolen, cheated, lied. I was despicable so far as my treatment to my parents was concerned. I married, and due to my selfish, brutal nature, I did not hold my wife. . . . As I grew older I saw the folly of my ways and reformed, but I could never rise above mediocrity so far as job and income was concerned. Your broadcast regarding forgiveness, and particularly forgiving one's self, opened my eyes. I realized how much I despised myself. I could hardly stand looking at myself in the mirror while shaving. You told how one could profit by his mistakes of the past and actually make this world a better place in which to live, due to past mistakes.

"Had I been near to you at the time I could have embraced you. Your words seemed to inject new life into a physical frame rapidly disintegrating through self-hatred.

"I did forgive myself, and prayed to the God above to help me keep the pledge I made to myself. My prayers were answered because from that day on I began to climb. I rose rapidly in the company with which I was working and have since acquired an interest in it. My future is bright and getting brighter. It is all due to my having cleansed my heart of the feeling I had held toward myself.

"Yes, I sometimes blush when I think of my escapades of the past, yet, in a way, I am grateful for them. It is through the life I led which has given me an appreciation for what I am now accomplishing.

"As to my marital status. Well, it was hard to convince her, but I did succeed in winning back the love and respect of the wife who couldn't stand me as I was. We are more than happy, and both of us feel eternally grateful to you."

STEP TWO. If you were to acquire the management of a business which had not been doing too well—what would you first do? You would make a comprehensive study of all phases of the enterprise. You would be interested in learning of the negative aspects of the business— those conditions which have been holding it back. Then you would look into the positive side, studying the angles which have kept the business alive. After your investigation, you would determine to minimize the negative characteristics—and amplify the positive ones.

Now that you are working toward the acquisition of self-mastery, you will want to do the same thing regarding your own being. You will want to know the negative traits so that you may lay out a program tending to eliminate them. You will want to know your good traits so that you may add to them.

Step Two, therefore, is to make an analysis of self. It would be well to put in writing the result of your self-study. Take a sheet of paper and draw a line down the center. On one side list all of your negative qualities; those traits you would like to minimize or eliminate. If you are timid, bashful or shy, make a note of it. If you worry to any extent, note that, too. If habits are proving a handicap, realize that self-mastery means controlling habits as well as other things—so specify your habits on the negative column of your self-analysis sheet.

Do you lack the art of conversation because you are a poor talker? If so, note the fact. Are you envious of others; are you jealous? You must master those traits, so add them to your list. Are you argumentative; do you frequently complain? Are you selfish? How about honesty and fair dealing? If you feel this is a sensitive spot with you, on your sheet reveal that you haven't been entirely fair and honest.

Probably the thoughts here given will not apply to you— they have been given merely as thought-starters. The idea is to list on the negative column of your sheet all of those characteristics which you consider as drawbacks.

Filling out the positive side will be more pleasant. Think of all of your desirable traits and list them. No, it will not be egotistical to recognize good things about yourself. You are working on a program of self-mastery, and this phase of it is necessary.

If you have a good disposition, fine—write it down. Ambition is a desirable trait and if you have it, list it. Just as you found it easy to think of negative qualities, so, too, will you find a long list of positive ones.

Reliability, alertness, cleanliness, honesty are just a few of the good things you might find regarding yourself, and, of course, they should be added to your list.

It is not my intention to name all of the good or bad traits. Just enough are given to enable you to carry on with your analysis so that you will have a picture of yourself as you are now—and be enabled to take the steps leading to self-mastery.

STEP THREE.   Probably the result of your following the suggestion in Step Two will be a revelation to you. You will have found that you are not such a bad person after all. Although you might have thought of many undesirable traits—they were more than offset by the items you were able to place in the positive column.

This step is to form a plan of action which will enable you to overcome the negative tendencies—and add to your good qualities.

Do not try to accomplish wonders over night. You spent many years, perhaps, in arriving at the place where you now find yourself—so expect to spend a short time, at least, in changing the picture.

Lay greatest stress to the negative column because each time you overcome a negative you automatically enhance the positives.

Carefully consider each item on your negative list and decide on which one you will work first. Do not take more than you can handle at a time. Some people might be able to work on all of them at once, but unless you feel perfectly safe in doing so, take just a few. And, after you determine to eliminate a negative, do not allow anything to defeat you. Determine that you will not stop short of complete victory. After you have eliminated the first selected negatives, then take some more to work on.

Paralleling your efforts on your negatives, you can also

be working on your positives. Take one or more of them and while you are going through the process of eliminating negatives, you can also be devoting time to enlarge on your positives.

STEP FOUR. This step should be carried on during the time you are working on the first three steps. To gain a consciousness of self-mastery, every time you think of it, repeat to yourself, thoughtfully:

"I am master of the thoughts I am thinking and the things I am doing. My future will be of my own making and will be a bright future, because I will do those things only which will assure a future of radiant health, prosperity—and happiness."

Every time you repeat these words to yourself, you will find something wonderful coming into your being. You will find great ease in conforming to the suggestions in the first steps and you will see yourself steadily climbing to the state where you *know*—beyond all doubt—that you are *master* of your own being.

CHAPTER TEN

Your Mental Yard-Stick

IF ALL OF the burners on the kitchen range were in use, and for some reason the cook wished to hasten the cooking of a certain item, she would most likely turn on more heat under that particular pot or pan. In Chapter Three of this book you were asked to make a pattern of the future you would like by listing *all* your objectives. Now suppose, for some reason, you would like to hasten the manifestation of some *specific objective*—you would like to know how to figuratively *turn on the heat* under that objective and hasten its entry into a state of being.

In this chapter you will be given a tool which can prove to be one of your most valuable possessions. I call it the *MENTAL YARD-STICK*. You will call it a *Magic Wand*. If you will use this tool every time you wish to accomplish anything, your chances of failure will be minimized and your chances for success tremendously magnified.

When I first began broadcasting over a New York station, I devoted a program in talking about the *MENTAL YARD-STICK*. A listener wrote, telling me that if he had known this principle ten years previous to that time, he would be wealthy. He said that in applying the *YARD-STICK* to his past undertakings, he could see *why* he *failed*—and how he could have *prevented* failure.

After you have finished this chapter, so that *you too* can appreciate its value, apply it to any one of your past undertakings. You will readily see *why you succeeded*, or *why you failed*. You will then thrill in knowing that you now possess a means of practically assuring the success of any contemplated venture; how you may acquire more and better possessions; how you may solve the most *perplexing* problems.

If you were an engineer and were given an assignment to design a bridge to span a river, what steps would you take first? You would want to learn everything about the conditions which exist *now*, wouldn't you? You would not only want the measurements showing the width of the river, but you would learn something of the earth-conditions on both sides of the river—where the bridge-towers would be constructed. If a tower should be required in midstream, you would ascertain the depth of the river at that point and the condition of the bed of the river—whether sand, silt or rock. After you had gained all the facts regarding conditions as they are *now*—you would be in a position to begin working up your plans for the bridge.

This illustration gives you the foundation of the *MENTAL YARD-STICK*—which I will now explain.

Just as a lineal yard has three parts, or feet, the *MENTAL YARD-STICK* has three parts—or, shall we say, phases.

The first phase of the *MENTAL YARD-STICK* is your *OBJECTIVE*.

The second phase, the *RESISTANCES* which stand between you and the attainment of your *OBJECTIVE*.

The third phase, the *PLAN OF ACTION* which will enable you to hurdle the *RESISTANCES* and attain your *OBJECTIVE*.

How to Use the Mental Yard-Stick!

THE OBJECTIVE. As strange as it may seem, very few people really know what they want in life. They might not be exactly satisfied with things as they are, but when you ask them, specifically, what they want, you will invariably get a vague answer. In using this *MENTAL YARD-STICK, you must be specific* so far as your objective is concerned. *KNOW JUST WHAT YOU WANT.*

If you are not satisfied with your job and want a better one—be *specific* and *know* what kind of a job you want; in fact, the type of a concern you would like to be associated with. Have the job so *clearly pictured* in your *mind* that you can *actually visualize yourself* as already working in it.

If your objective should be a business of your own—what kind of business? *Manufacturing, wholesaling, retailing?* Be *specific. SEE* in your mental pictures the business you would like to have.

If your objective should be a home—*what kind of a home?* And where? Draw a mental picture of the exact type of a home you would like to have.

Do you want friends? All right—that will be your objective. But here again, be *specific*—what *kind* of friends? Naturally, you will want friends with whom you will have something in common—music, literature, hobbies, etc.

RESISTANCES. After you have your objective, you *next* list *every* resistance which stands between you and the attainment of your objective. Do not list them *mentally,* but *write* them down. This gives you a clear mental picture of your problems before you. Then you are ready for the third and final phase of the *YARD-STICK.*

PLAN OF ACTION. If you have a clearly defined objective; if you have listed every resistance you can think of which stands between you and your objective—it is more than likely that your *PLAN OF ACTION* will be *effective.*

If you will study failures—and what caused them—you will invariably find that one or more of these three phases had been overlooked—usually the second one. We might have an objective—and we might attempt a *Plan of Action* to attain that objective—but, if we fail to consider all resistances when the *Plan of Action* is put into operation, we encounter a resistance not originally considered, and are *blocked.* If we consider all resistances beforehand, then our plan of action will be complete and will automatically take care of the resistances as they come up.

*   *   *

Getting back to the example of the engineer designing a bridge, we can now see that, using the *MENTAL YARD-STICK, we are just as scientific as the engineer.* In the illustration, the *bridge* would be the objective and, naturally, the engineer would be *specific* so far as the objective is concerned. He would know what kind of a bridge he wanted to design. His study of existing conditions, such as are found on both banks of the river, as well as study of the riverbed, would be to *uncover the RESISTANCES.* Then the design of the bridge, based on existing conditions, is the engineer's *PLAN OF ACTION.*

Salesmen can use this *MENTAL YARD-STICK* to very good advantage. In this connection, the *sale itself* becomes the *objective.* The *resistances* are the many *reasons* a prospect might advance for not wishing to make a purchase, and the *Plan of Action* would be the *sales solicitation* the salesman would use in overcoming the *RESISTANCES.*

The next two pages graphically show the *MENTAL YARD-STICK* in operation. One illustration shows the objective being a desire to learn the profession of *SALESMANSHIP.* The second illustration takes as an objective the acquiring of a *career* in the field of *writing.* Study these diagrams very carefully and then make a diagram of your own and apply the *MENTAL YARD-STICK* on *OBJECTIVES* of *YOUR OWN.*

Major and Minor Objectives

There are times when the objective will appear so monumental, it will be hard for one to visualize himself as attaining it. For example: he may have a good idea for a new kitchen gadget; something which could be used to advantage in every home.

The objective might be national distribution. The creator of the idea might visualize the time when his product would be on sale in most stores throughout the United

OBJECTIVE	GETTING A POSITION AS A SALESMAN

RESISTANCES	PLAN OF ACTION
Lack of knowledge regarding salesmanship	1: There are many magazines devoted to selling, as well as numerous good books. It is also possible to learn the fundamentals of selling through home study courses.
Lack of experience in selling	2: There are always opportunities for the person willing to sell on a commission basis. Spare time could be used for selling some item until experience is gained.
Lack of contacts with possible employers	3: First decide on the type of product you would like to sell—then build up a list of all companies making or distributing such items.
Lack of finances for special education	4: $1 will open a savings account in any bank. Laying aside just a few dollars weekly will grow into a sizeable sum in a short time.
How to seek a job after training is gained	5: Apply principles of salesmanship in letters to prospective employers—then SELL your services.

OBJECTIVE   RESISTANCES   PLAN OF ACTION

OBJECTIVE — TAKING UP A CAREER AS WRITER

RESISTANCES

Lack of knowledge of technique of writing.

Inability to properly express myself.

Insufficient time for study and practice.

Lack of finances for instruction.

Fear of scoffing and criticism of relatives and friends if new career is attempted.

How to dispose of stories after becoming a writer.

PLAN OF ACTION

1. There are many good books on writing and journalism available. Also, it is possible to study writing at night school or through a home study course.

2. This may also be learned as above. Too, the moment you become *expression conscious* you will begin to improve as you will watch your own expression and study it in the works of others.

3. We all have all the time there is. No one has a minute more than you have. No matter how busy one might think he is, or appears to be, — he can always manage to adjust his work so that he may find time to do the things he *really wants to do*.

4. *Desire will find a way*. As soon as you generate sufficient enthusiasm for your objective, you will find the needed money either through an adjustment of your budget, or by acquiring extra money through overtime or side-work.

5. Scoffing and criticism can spur you on if you accept it as a challenge to prove that you can really do the things you set out to do.

6. Editors and publishers are constantly on the lookout for new writers to replace those who are always dropping out of the field. Manuscripts of unknown writers are considered. If your script comes back — re-write it and send it to another publisher — and so on until you *click*.

This yard stick is very important. Study it carefully.

Ben Sweetland

States. At the time, he may have nothing more than the idea. In such a position, it would require quite a stretch of the imagination for this man to see himself in such an ideal position when he realizes the tremendous sums of money necessary for factories, machinery, raw materials, etc. Even this is not all. It is no longer surprising to hear of advertising campaigns running into millions of dollars annually. So, the objective grows into staggering proportions as one thinks through on it.

In such an instance, it would be difficult for the average person to apply the Mental Yard-Stick. It would be hard to lay out a plan of action, because reaching the objective would appear as a long, tedious climb.

With problems of this kind, it is suggested to work with major and minor objectives. This means that the objective would become a *Major Objective,* and this would be broken down into a series of *Minor Objectives.*

This book is being written in the San Francisco Bay Area, so we will give the illustration using this part of the country as the starting point.

If you take a map of the United States and put your finger on San Francisco, you would see that the amount of space it occupies in comparison with the entire country is infinitesimal.

All right, let us consider the development of the San Francisco Bay Area Market as the Minor Objective. This will be simple compared with the entire country. For this small market, perhaps a local manufacturer can be prevailed upon to manufacture the item upon a reasonable basis. This would eliminate the necessity of a factory and machinery, for the time being, at least. It could well be possible to get someone to put up a small amount of capital for an interest in the venture. This money could be used for local advertising. It is simple to see that this first Minor Objective would not be hard to attain. Incidentally, in handling a Minor Objective, do so just as if it were your Major Objective. In fact, until that objective is attained, it is the only one you are to consider. With the Minor, you consider the *resistances*—and the *plan of action* for that specific objective.

Your next objective might be the State of California, and, with the start already made, this should not prove too difficult. Remember, you follow through on each minor just as though it were a major for the time being.

The third objective could be the three western States; then a jump could be made including all of the western States up to the Great Divide. From there you might go as far as the Mississippi, and continue to add territory until your Major Objective is reached—National distribution.

The history of many of our largest companies follows this pattern. Vick's Vapo-Rub, for example, was born in a small kitchen in Atlanta, Georgia, and the immediate neighborhood was the initial market. That product can now be found in every town and hamlet throughout the civilized world.

A woman once bemoaned the fact that she would like to play the piano, but she could never go through the tortuous grind of working on so many elementary lessons before reaching the point where she would be able to produce listenable music.

The principles of the Major and Minor Objectives were

outlined to her, and she was asked to consider the *ability to play well* as her *Major Objective,* but to think of each individual lesson as a Minor Objective.

"Suppose you had nothing to do except to complete the work on an individual lesson, would it be difficult?" she was asked. Her answer, of course, was "no". She admitted it would be simple to take just one lesson and become perfect in playing the exercises just as instructed.

I suggested to her that in the future she think of her work as *a lesson at a time* and give no thought at all to any to be given in the future. She should take each lesson with the attitude that there was nothing else to it.

A few months later, with an enthusiastic smile, she said, "I know it is just kidding myself, but your plan works. I am making wonderful progress with my music and it is really fun, not work."

THE HALF WAY MARK!

As you complete this chapter you have reached the half way mark in your acceptance of life's golden secrets. Were you to stop right now and continue no further, you would not be able to appraise in terms of dollars and cents what this work can mean to you; that is, if you have been *think-ing* while reading.

I will not be happy with mere mediocre results, how-ever. I want you to get the full value of all this book offers —so I have an important suggestion to make.

Do not begin on Section II until you review this entire section. Start with Chapter One and, before reading it, close your eyes and recall to mind as much as you can of what you learned in that chapter. After you have done so, re-read the chapter, slowly and thoughtfully. As much as you may have gained the first time, you will be pleased and surprised to find out how much more you will be able to obtain from the second reading.

Do this with each chapter until you reach the one you have just completed. As enthusiastic as you may have become so far, you will find it still mounting. You will then approach the Second Section with an eagerness born from the visions of a life more abundant which has been, and is, unfolding for you.

There is now more meaning behind the two simple words: "I Can!"

SECTION TWO

How to Focus Your Powers for the Attainment of Specific Objectives

CHAPTER ELEVEN

Personality and How to Build a Magnetic One

THIS IS GOING to be a "conversational" chapter. I mean by that—instead of feeling that I am writing, I will think of myself as sitting with you, informally, explaining the fundamentals which enter into the making of a *MAGNETIC PERSONALITY*.

Perhaps it may seem like a big assignment on my part to attempt to cover, in a few pages, a subject as comprehensive as *PERSONALITY*.

You know, a package of seeds is so small that it could almost be lost in your pocket or your handbag; still, with this package of seeds, it is possible to create a large garden of most glorious blossoms. I want you to think of this chapter in the same light as you would consider a package of seeds; but its contents will be seeds of thought; seeds which, if properly planted and cultivated, will result in the blossoming of a personality so radiantly magnetic people will be drawn toward you—*and like you.*

All right—first of all, let us think about a *magnetic personality,* so we will know just what a *magnetic personality* really is. You know, we cannot start to build something until we have a definite idea as to what we want to build; and then, after we know this, we must have a plan from which to work.

A *MAGNETIC PERSONALITY* is *not* something we can see—but something we *feel*. Remember this: It makes no difference whether you are tall or short, lean or fat, dark or light; you will find, as you read further, that it is possible for *everyone,* regardless of his or her present physical make-up, to develop a *MAGNETIC PERSONALITY*.

Among your acquaintances, haven't you found those who are not pleasant to be with? They might be well educated; they might dress well; they might have money; yet, there is something about them which makes you uncomfortable when you are in their presence. You may not be able to determine just why, but a little of them goes a long way. You feel inwardly happy when the visit is over. On the other hand, can't you think of those whose presence is most welcome? Again, you may not be able to determine just *why*. They might not be quite as well educated as the others, they might have less of the worldly goods—yet, you feel comfortable when you are with them and enjoy every minute. Why is this? It is because one group has developed that unseen something I refer to as a *MAGNETIC PERSONALITY—the other group has NOT.*

In considering our physical characteristics, as pertaining to a *magnetic personality,* I am not overlooking the importance of good health. Good health *is* important—vitally so. But, you will discover, to your amazement, that, as your personality grows, your health will improve. You will put the *constructive* laws of Nature to work for you—which, in turn, will have a definite rejuvenation effect on your entire being.

You will begin thinking in terms of health and strength and vitality. You will feel a definite urge to select your foods wisely. You will want to take full advantage of the *God given* energy contained in every breath of fresh air and every ray of sunshine. You will see to it that every fibre in your being is kept sufficiently active, so that they will remain supple—and alive. You will plan your days and nights so that you will have proper rest and relaxation; giving Nature full opportunity to restore and renew all worn tissue. In fact, the step you are about to take will be the beginning of a great transformation. From your present physical frame, which perhaps has housed pains and aches, worry and fear, gloom and sorrow; like the *Phoenix from the ashes,* will arise a new self—vibrantly alive, radiantly magnetic, and gloriously happy. Have I aroused your imagination? Can't you already glimpse the dawn of a new day?

This chapter is going to prove more than a few printed pages to you. It will prove to be the *talisman* which will take you by the hand and lead you into a new world. Heretofore, you have read books—many good ones—but they were just books to you. Each one added new knowledge to your mental storehouse; but that was *all.* This time it will be different. You wouldn't have purchased this book if you hadn't had a desire to improve yourself. You wouldn't now study this chapter if the desire were not still present. So, as you read, each thought expressed will act as an energy impulse spurring you on to the attainment of your *OBJECTIVE.*

Everyone has a personality which creates an impression on those with whom he comes in contact. But, there are two types of personalities: the one which attracts people to you—*magnetic*—and the one which repels. Both types of personality are the result of the kind of thinking which has been implanted in the *CREATIVE MIND* through the *CONSCIOUS MIND.* So, since it is your earnest desire to have a *MAGNETIC PERSONALITY,* you will find that, by accepting the thoughts to follow, a *magnetic personality* will not only be easy to acquire—but soon be an established *fact.*

Up to this point, I have made the picture of a *MAGNETIC PERSONALITY* so alluring, you may have gained the impression that to attain one requires weeks, months, or perhaps years of laborious work. If so, you will be prepared for a pleasant surprise; because the building of a *MAGNETIC PERSONALITY* is simplicity itself. So simple, in fact, one may have a tendency to doubt the efficacy of the suggestions which follow. But, if you will become analytical for a moment, you'll agree wholeheartedly with the soundness of these principles; and you will instinctively know, that by applying them, you'll gain reward. All right—let's consider the elements which tend toward making, or detracting from, a *MAGNETIC PERSONALITY.* And remember, as you proceed, you are not going to think of this chapter as something prepared for many, but as a special message for you—*AND YOU ALONE.*

*   *   *

TIMIDITY. There are very few things which detract more from a likable personality than *TIMIDITY* and

SHYNESS. Yet, when one understands the principles, it is almost as easy to eliminate *timidity* as it is to erase chalk from a blackboard.

In most cases, *timidity* is a condition created during our childhood. The parent plants thoughts in the mind of a child to the effect that he is *shy* or *timid,* and these thoughts, being accepted by the *CREATIVE MIND,* are *retained* throughout life; at least, until the timid individual learns how to replace these *negative* thoughts with *positive* ones.

Overcoming *TIMIDITY* is merely a question of re-educating the *CREATIVE MIND.* If you have been holding to thoughts such as "I am timid", "I am shy", etc., all you will have to do is to replace such thoughts with those of *courage, strength* and *power.* It may seem a bit incongruous to you for me to suggest that you say to yourself you have courage, when up to now you know you have been timid; but with what you have learned regarding the *CREATIVE MIND,* you can easily understand the reason for doing so. Each time you give expression to the thought that you are timid, you have actually instructed your *CREATIVE MIND* to create a condition of *timidity* within your being. Each time you make the statement: "I am brave", you are instructing your *CREATIVE MIND* to create within yourself a condition of *bravery.* And, permit me to offer this warning: When you apply this principle, do not *watch* for results; just *KNOW* that they are there. You cannot see a seed develop into a plant, yet you *KNOW* that, when you plant and properly cultivate it, a plant will result. This fundamental I have given you is as basic as the law of mathematics. If you plant the *POSI-*

TIVE THOUGHT in your mind and adhere to it, just like the unfolding plant you will find that your *timidity* will vanish and be replaced with strength and courage.

When you are with others, do not feel inferior due to lack of education or lack of material wealth. Be proud of everything you *have* and *are*—and *KNOW* that it is just as much a privilege for others to know *you* as it is for you to know *them.*

In talking about *timidity,* I am not advocating that you develop the opposite trait—that of boldness. One can be as bad as the other. The condition you are to create for yourself is one whereby you'll be at ease when you are with others. You will be able to retain your own self-respect as well as gain the respect of those with whom you will be brought into contact.

FEAR.   Did you ever see a man or woman with a *MAGNETIC PERSONALITY who had a mind filled with fear?* I haven't. The two just do not go together. So, the next point we must consider is the *elimination* of fear. Fear brings about a state of mental paralysis which actually *prevents* one from taking the steps which would enable him to overcome the condition which caused the fear. And, how can you overcome fear? Well, it is easier than you might, at this moment, imagine. Just use your reasoning faculties a bit. What is it that you are fearing? Is it fear that you will lose your job? Fear will not help, will it? It will prevent you from doing your best work—thereby giving reason for that which you fear to become a reality. Are you fearing the possible consequence of an illness? If this is the case—now that you *know* something about the operation of the *CREATIVE MIND*—you will understand that to hold fear thoughts will actually aggravate the condition and make it worse instead of helping Nature to make you well. In fact, you can overcome fear in the same way you overcome *timidity*. *Each time a FEAR THOUGHT* enters your head, think a bit. *KNOW* that from *FEAR* nothing but *harm* can come. As you find your *strength* and *power* increasing, you will have little or no difficulty in correcting the condition which might have *caused* the *fear*.

WORRY. How can *worry detract* from a *magnetic personality?* Permit me to ask you a question. Are you drawn to the person whose face reveals a mind of worry? Please do not misunderstand me. I am not being cold and unsympathetic. I am merely trying to point out the fallacy of worry.

In addition to the rules given in Chapter Seven regarding Worry, let us think of this enemy as it applies to Personality.

For a moment, think of worry regarding business and financial conditions. If a person has allowed himself to become low mentally through financial troubles, the *face* he presents will not be one which would inspire *confidence* that he could stage a *successful* comeback. While others might be sympathetic, they will feel that he has gone *down for the count* and hasn't the stamina to fight his way back. I knew a man who was backed in the corner so far with financial difficulties, it looked like only a *miracle* would extricate him. But he had *faith* in *himself*. He *knew* that if he could present a front of *courageousness* and *determination,* he would reach victory. And, without the world knowing anything of his troubles, he carried onward. One by one he surmounted his obstacles, and is now facing a future of genuine happiness. Suppose this man had done nothing except spend his time in *worry?* He would probably be living on charity and feeling cynical about this thing we call life. So, agreeing with me that *worry* can do nothing but *harm you,* for the sake of your *happiness* and the *MAGNETIC PERSONALITY* you are about to acquire—*eliminate it.*

SELF-PITY. Now I *have* brought up a ticklish subject. *Self-pity* is something indulged in by most people—yet only few admit it. But, fortunately, in your self-analysis you don't have to admit to others what you find. Just as *timidity* is often started during childhood, so too is *self-pity* a trait we develop in our early years. The mother who is always showering sympathy on little Mary for every bruise or scratch, without realizing it, is creating a situation whereby little Mary will grow into womanhood carrying with her an abundance of *self-pity.*

Do you enjoy being with an individual who is constantly complaining about aches and pains and worries of all kinds, and who does so merely to gain your sympathy? I don't think so. You are a bit relieved when the visit with such a person has ended. Well, think a little to discover whether or not *you* are ever guilty of so annoying others. Isn't it far better to have people rejoice with you than to feel sorry for you? I'm certain you agree.

During a period of business depression, a salesman came to me feeling very sorry for himself because his business was so bad. In fact, he really had no business at all. He just couldn't close any orders. I asked him if he constantly talked about bad business when with prospects. He looked at me and said: "Well, when they ask me how business is, I cannot lie and say it is *good* when I'm not getting a single order." I told him what he could say, and he would be telling the gospel truth. Instead of moaning about bad business, he could tell others that he had *never* been *busier* in his life. And, if he was working as hard as he should in getting business, this could easily be true. Well, this man got the point. A few days later he came into my office actually beaming. "It works," was his first remark. He told me that executives really found it refreshing to meet a man who was *doing* things, instead of constantly grumbling about bad conditions. Soon the depression had *ended* so far as *this man* was concerned—and mainly because he had eliminated *SELF-PITY* from his make-up.

Have *you* ever indulged in *SELF-PITY?* If so, remember this: Just as you resent constant complaining from others, so too will they resent it in you. The elimination of *self-pity* is a very definite step toward the attainment of a *MAGNETIC PERSONALITY.* To prove this is true. think back a bit over your method of selecting friends. For example, when you make up a list of guests for a party, don't you say something like this: "Now let's see, I'll ask Mr. Jones, he is very interesting. Oh yes, I want Mrs. Brown, she always adds so much to a party. No, I'll not ask Mrs. Smith. She's nice—but she is a wet blanket. She's always complaining about something." Isn't this true? Certainly. So, if you blush a bit and discover that you have been guilty of *self-pity at times—eliminate it right now.*

CONSIDERATION FOR OTHERS.   Now I am going to touch on a subject which, at first, may seem unimportant.

The late Elbert Hubbard made a very interesting statement, when he said: "I love you because you love the things I love." Just analyze this thought a moment and you will gain its real significance. If you are exhibiting some possession, of which you are justly proud, how do you like to have your guest tell you how much *better* it might be— or mention a friend or relative who has a better one? Doesn't it almost cause you to say naughty words under your breath? On the other hand, doesn't it bring a warm glow of friendship to your heart if your guest shows proper appreciation for that which you have been showing? Now you will more fully understand what Hubbard meant when he said: "I love you because you love the things I love."

Tardiness is another way of showing *lack of consideration for others.* When you're late for appointments, you have *actually robbed* the other fellow of part of his time. And if you think this has no bearing on a *MAGNETIC PERSONALITY,* just recall to your mind the times you have waited on cold or windy corners for a tardy one to show up—and see if the tardiness made you think as much of the person as you otherwise might do.

Then here is another question. When you call upon someone and you find that he or she is busy, do you continue to remain? If you find a person very busy and there is nothing you can do to assist you will be adding to your popularity by making a quick and graceful exit. Your consideration for others will be appreciated and will be *re-*

flected in the closer bond of friendship which will later exist.

This thought of consideration for others could be carried on for several pages, but enough has been given to aid you in your *SELF-ANALYSIS*.

MAKING FRIENDS. I have often made the statement to the effect that to *have* a friend you must *be* a friend. I want you to think about this statement a moment—and the more you think about it, the more you will gain from it. Do you think of friends as people from whom you can gain *favors?* If you do, I can tell you right now that you haven't many friends. If you meet someone whom you'd like to have as a friend, *forget entirely* about the aid you might gain from that individual, but do think of all the things you can do to make that person a bit happier in life. Soon you will discover a new friendship is developing. Some might say: "Well, why should I make a friend if I am to do *all* the *giving?* Those who feel this way have *not yet* learned the true meaning of the word *FRIEND.*

We do things for our friends because they *are* our friends, and we *enjoy* performing any act which will add to their happiness. We do not do it merely for what we get in return, except for the happiness we may have gained by making another happy. But here is a strange thing! When we *unselfishly* do things to make others happy, they —when the opportunity presents itself—will do things to make us happy.

Here is something else to remember! In business, you know, concerns have what they call *assets* and *liabilities*. Too many liabilities will wreck any business. Well, in life we might call our friends *assets* and our enemies *liabilities.*

Just as too many liabilities will ruin a business, so will too many enemies destroy a person's happiness. If you have any enemies, now is a good time to begin thinking of everything you can do to win the friendship of these enemies. Each time you do this, you are making a double gain. You have reduced your liabilities and *increased* your *assets*.

FORGIVENESS. Here is something which is so important you cannot afford to overlook it; that is, if you sincerely intend to create for yourself a *MAGNETIC PERSONALITY.* Whenever you do anything to injure another, are you big enough to ask forgiveness? When another injures you, are you big enough to forgive? Do you know that you cannot afford to maintain hatred or ill-will in your heart? Hatred actually creates a poison in the system which is detrimental to health. To prove whether or not I am right, just think of someone you know who is called a *sour-puss;* a person who is against everything and everybody. Is that person in good health? Doesn't he or she constantly complain about pains and aches? And poor health is not the only effect of a *sour-puss* disposition. Hatred will carve hard lines on the face. The eyes become cold and piercing. The mouth is not friendly. The voice lacks warmth. So you can imagine how all of this would go with a *MAGNETIC PERSONALITY. It would be like mixing oil with water.*

BAD MANNERISMS. What I am about to say might seem a contradiction to what I said in the beginning of this chapter. I said: "Personality is something we *feel,* but do not *see.*" We do see—and feel—bad mannerisms. And bad mannerisms will *mar* an otherwise fine personality, just as a poorly selected frame will detract from a beautiful painting.

One time, during a broadcast on *PERSONALITY* and *HOW TO BUILD A MAGNETIC ONE,* I put on a little impromptu contest in which I offered simple prizes for the longest lists of bad mannerisms. This is hard to believe, but some lists contained over three hundred of them. The lists included all sorts of bad mannerisms, such as: nail-biting, finger-tapping, poking others with your fingers to make sure they are listening, picking at the nose, butting in, inattention, etc. You can think of dozens more, and as you do so, you will realize that they do not help at all toward the building of a *MAGNETIC PERSONALITY.* So watch others for the things you do not consider as becoming and then study yourself to see whether or not you too might be guilty of doing the same things. If you are, then you have learned something else to do in order to improve your own personality.

I told you that this chapter should be looked at in the light of a packet of seeds—seeds of thought. What I have attempted to do is to make you *PERSONALITY CONSCIOUS.* If I have succeeded in doing this, the time you have spent on these pages will pay you huge dividends. Begin *now* with studying yourself. Never reach the point where you are satisfied with your own personality. *KNOW* that it is improving—and that day by day it is getting *better and better.* It will not be long before friends and relatives will marvel at your transformation.

CHAPTER TWELVE

125—Your Normal Life Span

THIS TIME, LET's be different. Ordinarily, when reading an article which advances a new theory, you are asked to be credulous, or, at least, you are expected to keep an open mind until after you have completed it. The reverse will hold true with this one. You are asked to read this chapter with genuine skepticism. In fact, you should acquire such a skeptical attitude you will not be content to accept any theory given without first proving the soundness of it to your own satisfaction. It is then the sincere hope of the author that through your investigation something fine will come into your life which will not only prolong it, but add immeasurably to your happiness during the period you remain on this earth.

It is my belief, and my conviction is strengthened by the opinions of many of our great scientists, that the normal life expectancy of man should be at least 125 years. It is the purpose of this chapter to prove this is true; to show why human beings are not now reaching this natural age—and to point out ways and means whereby we may attain the age intended for us.

Human beings mature physically at varying ages, usually between 16 and 20 years; yet, except in rare cases are they mentally mature much before the age of fifty. But when we do reach the age of fifty, we begin preparing for death. This statement may seem a bit startling at first, but as you read further you will find it to be true. As I say these things, I am speaking in generalities, of course. There are exceptions which prove the rule. When we think of people who have passed the age of fifty, we refer to them as being old, or at least rather well along in years. When we, ourselves, pass fifty, we begin to look at ourselves as being old. We hesitate taking up anything new especially if it may require a period of five, ten, or fifteen years, thinking that we are too old to make such an attempt. At the close of spring each year, salesmen—and even merchants—will begin to prepare for a summer of poor business—and they are never disappointed. They do have a poor summer, and why shouldn't they. They prepared for it. So, too, with human beings regarding age. At the age of fifty they begin to let down, with the thoughts of the rapidly approaching 60's or 70's in mind. An ache or a pain which would not be noticed in early life is accepted as a certain indication of age. Then we are subjected to the well-meaning suggestions of friends. We are urged not to do this and not to do that, because "we are not as young as we used to be." In other words, everything possible is done by ourselves and others to give us an age consciousness. And, what a pity. We have to live to an age of fifty before we really reach a stage of full mental maturity. Our first twenty years are spent in growing out of childhood and gaining our primary education. Between twenty and thirty we begin "trying our wings" in getting an idea what this life is all about. From thirty to forty, if we are fortunate, we become more or less settled in the work we intend to follow. The years from forty to fifty are spent in gaining experience. Then . . . ? We awake to the realization we are old. We have spent fifty years in preparation. Preparation for what? Does this seem to be the life Nature intended for us? I think not. Let us look into Nature a bit and think about the span of life allotted to forms of life other than that of human beings. A dog, for example, reaches maturity at the age of one year; he lives an average age of 10 years—or ten times the period between birth and maturity. The average age of all living creatures, except human beings, is at least seven times the period of elapsed time between birth and maturity.

Is Nature inconsistent? Did she intend a certain life span for all common forms of life—and for human beings, the highest form of all life—a life span of less than half that of the shortest lived creature? Certainly not. And it will be the intention of this chapter to prove that the normal life span of man is at least 125 years; and that, if we live and think as Nature intended we should, we, too, can reach this rightful age.

In Hollywood, I received a letter from a man of 56 who had given up hopes of ever being of further use to humanity. He had been successful in his life, but through bad guessing in the market, his money had vanished. He felt too old to get another job—or to make a new start in life. His wife departed to live with a married daughter in the east and he remained with a son who was supporting him.

Listening to my radio talks on age, and hearing that the normal span of life for man should be at least 125 years, caused him to do a bit of serious thinking. He realized, if he was to live to be that old, that he, at 56, was really a young man just in the prime of his life. He emerged from the lethargy he had allowed himself to get into, and with new hope and courage, began to remould his new life. The last report I had from this man was indeed an inspiration. He had interested a few friends in a business venture and was already getting away to a good start. He is now arranging a home, so that he and his wife can be re-united.

Do you know how the expression "feeling up to par" originated? An Englishman by the name of Thomas Parr was born in Winnington, Shropshire, in the year 1483. This man, at the age of 130, was still physically fit to thresh his own corn. In 1635 his fame had reached Thomas Howard, 2nd Earl of Arundel, who invited him to London. Here he was presented to King Charles I, but the change of air and diet soon affected him and he died at Lord Arundel's house in London on November 14, 1635. He was buried in the south transept of Westminster Abbey. This man reached an age of 152 years. But he was not an exception. Thomas Parr had a son who reached the age of 125 years, and he would probably have reached a much older age had his life not been cut short through an accident. So, in the future, when you use the expression "feeling up to par," you will virtually be admitting that you have lost your age consciousness and are feeling like the man who did reach his normal expectancy in life.

At present, the average individual actually begins preparing for death at the age of fifty. It is easy to understand why this is true. Feeling that life is better than two thirds gone, we see ourselves too rapidly approaching the end. We begin to live in the past instead of the future. We consider our bodies as partially worn out pieces of machinery and we hesitate to attempt any kind of normal activity for fear that the "old" machine will falter and stop functioning. Now then, imagine that you knew definitely your normal span of life was at least 125 years—how would you feel at fifty? Would you feel old? Of course not. You would realize that you had just passed through the first fifty years of your life which had prepared you, mentally and physically, for another fifty years of real constructive activity.

Man's period of life between fifty and one hundred should be the most important years of his existence. It is during this time that he should be able to make the greatest contributions to humanity. The average intelligent man has to be at least fifty years old before he has really learned to know just how little he knows. I am saying this seriously. It takes real intelligence to fully appreciate how little we do know in comparison to that yet to be learned. Each time we delve into a new subject, we discover the tremendous amount of knowledge there is to be gained on it, and if it is a subject of interest, and we knew that we had man active years ahead of us, we would take delight in exploring the field and learning more about it.

On one occasion I was guest of honor at a banquet in a large mid-western city. I selected as a title for my talk the same one as I have given this chapter: "125—Your Normal

Life Span." The average ages of those present were from forty to sixty. At the end of my talk one man approached me and said: "Mr. Sweetland, in a few weeks I will be fifty. In my earlier days I always wanted to take up the study of microscopy, but then I could not afford a good microscope. Now that I can afford one I have hesitated, thinking I was too old. After hearing your talk this evening, I have decided to proceed on this study, and I know that in the future years I will not only learn a lot, but will gain a great deal of pleasure in doing so."

A very attractive lady from my audience came up to me and asked me how old I thought she was. Of course this is a dangerous question to answer, but after her insistence I told her that I thought she was in the neighborhood of forty-five—and I was sincere in my guess. She did not look a day over that age. Her eyes beamed when she told me she would be seventy on her next birthday. This woman owns and manages three large companies. She arises every morning at five and works diligently all day. She told me that she arrived in her city when she was fifty—and was penniless. Without realizing that she was operating along sound natural laws, she decided that she was not going to grow old and that she was going to make a success of life. She did, and according to her present physical condition, she will, barring accidents, of course, live her full span of life of at least 125 years.

If I should mention the word "rose," what would you see with your mind's eye? Would you see the letters r-o-s-e? No, just as you learned in Chapter Six, you would see the picture of a rose. This is because the mind does not think in terms of words, but pictures. Everything we see, hear or read, we translate into mental pictures. In other words, we "see" what we hear and read.

The Creative Mind is influenced by the thoughts of the conscious mind; if we hold negative thoughts, we will get a negative reaction; if we hold positive thoughts, we get a positive reaction. Keep this in mind because it is so important, as you will realize as you continue. Our mental pictures are really patterns used by the Creative Mind—just as a builder might use a blueprint.

Now then, let us think about the type of mental pictures we must maintain if we are sincere in our desire to reach our normal life span of 125.

Would you believe me if I should tell you that most of us lose our youth far too early in life, due entirely to the wrong kind of mental pictures?

First of all, I want to establish the fact that human beings do not live nearly as long as nature intended them to live. Yes, I know that the Bible tells us (Psa. 90.10) "The days of our years are threescore years and ten." If, however, we turn back to Genesis 6.3 we read "his (man's) days shall be a hundred and twenty years." I am not giving these quotations in an attempt to dispute the Bible. The discrepancy, if any, is undoubtedly due to our lack of understanding of time measurement at the time the statements were made. If we read Chapter Five of Genesis in its entirety, we find many references to men who lived from a hundred years up to Methuselah, who reached the age of 969 years.

Still referring to the Bible, we find an interesting thought in Proverbs 4.10. "Hear, O my son, and receive my sayings; and the years of thy life shall be many." As we read the Bible, we find that the essence of all of the teachings contained therein, is: "Live right: think right." If this interpretation is correct, then we can find much comfort in the quotation just given. We then have the promise which, in effect, assures us many added years if we accept—and abide by—the thoughts as outlined herein.

The life span of man, to be in keeping with all other forms of life on this earth, should be at least 125 years. Some scientists claim much more—even up to 200 years, but the minimum figure will give us a good objective, especially when we compare it with "threescore years and ten," which is 70 years.

It might be asked: "If we should have a life span of 125 years, why do we show signs of age around 50 and then die just a few years later?" And, of course, this is a good question.

In days gone by, most of the early deaths were attributed to lack of knowledge of hygiene, hardships, etc. The normal expectancy of life, at birth, has been increasing year after year, as human beings learn more regarding self-preservation.

Man has progressed in his mastery over the elements and germs. And, through the invention of labor-saving devices, has greatly simplified the art of living. And now, as we pass the half-way mark in the Twentieth Century, we are learning one of the most important secrets of life—the potency of MENTAL PICTURES.

Now I will answer the question: "Why do we become old at 50?" It is because we hold pictures of age. I'll return to this thought a bit later, but first I want to recall to mind a biological fact which has a definite bearing on this thought.

The body is made up of billions of cells. These cells are constantly being worn out and replaced with new cells. In a period of 11 months, most of the cells of the body have been replaced. In seven years, all of them have been replaced.

New cells are produced under the direction of our Creative Mind, and these cells use as a pattern the mental pictures of the Conscious Mind. Now I can give an explanation of the statement above to the effect that we grow old because we hold pictures of age.

Since we have accepted the thought that the normal life span of man is 70 years (threescore years and ten), it will not be difficult to understand why we begin to show signs of age so early in life. When we are passing through our forties, we are holding mental pictures of ourselves as we will look at fifty. When fifty arrives, we find the age-signs in our faces and bodies—because we have been putting them there. Our faithful Creative Mind has taken the mental picture and reproduced it in our physical beings. During our fifties, we maintain mental pictures as to how we should look at sixty; and when sixty arrives, we do look that age, and for the same reason.

Our mirrors are often very unfriendly to us. With many people, mirrors are responsible for the development of an age consciousness.

Usually when we go to the mirror we are alone. Our facial expression is generally serious as we examine our reflection in the mirror—because we are critical as to how we look. When we are serious, tiny lines and creases in the face become more noticeable, which add a worried note to the serious expression.

All right—what happens when we leave the mirror? We keep in mind the mental picture as to how we looked when we last saw ourselves. That mental picture becomes a pattern for the Creative Mind which proceeds to reproduce it in our physical being.

Your mirror can also work for you if you will permit it to do so. Step to your mirror right now and force yourself to look very happy. Think of something very pleasant, and *smile*. Do you see how much younger you look? And did you notice how much more attractive you are? All right— if you acquire the habit of looking *happy* each time you peer into the mirror—then you will be giving happy patterns to your Creative Mind. And you will notice continual improvement each time you see your reflection.

To create—*and possess*—youth, we must maintain mental pictures of youth. At this point it might be well to reach an understanding as to what we mean when we say *youth*. *In referring to youth, I mean that state of being where you really feel young, where you can enjoy the activity of youth, where your face shows that glad-to-be-alive sparkle of youth, and your mind is active and alert. This will be our objective regarding youth.*

In connection with the mental aspects of youth, I will give you five simple rules which, if followed, will put you well on the road toward acquiring them. Right now, take a pencil and underscore the words *if followed,* and know that merely reading these rules will not be enough; you must act upon them.

RULE ONE. Accept 125 years as your normal life

span and live accordingly. Lay out your life just as though you were given definite assurance that you would live to be at least 125 years of age. If you have had a desire to take up some new study, no matter what your present age might be, arrange to do so. Many people have successfully taken up painting, writing, music, science, etc., when in the sixties, seventies, and even eighties. The only time you are too old to learn is when you *think* you are too old.

RULE TWO.   Develop a *youth consciousness.* Think of yourself as being young—both in mind and body. Hold mental pictures of yourself in good health. Never think of yourself in any other way except as being young, because in reality your body is young. Remember, your cells are constantly renewing themselves, and if you hold mental pictures of youth and strength, the new cells will reflect your type of thinking.

RULE THREE.   Live in the future. Do you understand what is meant by this statement? Remember—you cannot relive the past. If you were more successful in the past than you are today, do not dwell upon it, and pity yourself because you are not doing as well today. Be grateful that you have had such experiences, and know that you have what it takes to do as well, if not better, in the future. If you made mistakes in the past, do not spend your time grieving over them. It will not help in the least, and will neutralize any possible good you may get from this chapter. *Live in the future.* If your work does not keep you fully occupied, take up a hobby of some kind; a hobby which will enlist your enthusiastic interest.

RULE FOUR.   Acquire a taste for the beautiful. Become *beauty conscious.* Train yourself to think in terms of beauty. Appreciate the beauty of the sunsets, the trees and flowers, the mountains and the ocean. Learn to dwell mentally on the things you like, instead of the things you do not like.

Make a friend of your mirror. Every time you glance at your reflection, carry a happy smile to your mirror and you will like the happy face which smiles back at you. Do not look into your mirror for signs of age. Look for signs of youth. Remember what you have already learned regarding mental pictures. If you hold to thoughts of yourself as becoming younger, you are supplying your Creative Mind with the proper pattern with which to work.

RULE FIVE. Knowledge is of no value unless you make use of it. Read these rules many times until you know them thoroughly. Then follow them, not once, or twice, but make them a part of your life. Most of our living is according to habit. We have good habits. We have bad habits. Make the living of these simple rules your future habit.

After a few weeks, when friends begin commenting on the change they see in you, it will then be easy to follow these thoughts because you will have an incentive. It is the first few weeks when you will have to prod yourself on so that you will reach the point where others will notice the great improvement.

Up to this point we have considered longevity from the psychological aspect. In other words, gaining an acceptance of the fact that man should reach an age of at least 125 years. Since, however, man is dual in his make-up, mental and physical, it will be necessary, if a long and exuberant life is desired, to consider *both* mind *and* body.

Follow a sane routine, such as that outlined in the fine book by Gaylord Hauser: "Look Younger—Live Longer." Make health your hobby so that you will follow a health pattern because it is fun to do so and not in the spirit of making sacrifices in order to prolong your life. As a matter of fact, there would be no point in extending our lives if we were to curtail our enjoyment through so doing.

As a final thought, from this moment onward, think of your possible life span as being 125 years and live accordingly. Doing this will mean that regardless what your present age might be—50, 60, 70, or even in the 80's—you are still young. Refuse to think of yourself as being old, and immediately discard any statements from others which might in any way refer to your present age as being old.

I am practicing what I preach and am feeling better, mentally and physically, than I have at any time during the past 30 years. You will soon be saying how much better—*and younger*—you feel.

CHAPTER THIRTEEN

How to Develop a Powerful Memory

LITERALLY SPEAKING, THERE is no such thing as a poor memory. It has been found that everything one reads and hears throughout his life is retained in the subconscious or Creative Mind.

"Why do we forget," one might ask, "if we retain everything we learn?"

You might know for a certainty that in your home there is a pair of scissors, yet you may not be able to lay your hands on them—they have been mislaid. This makes a good illustration so far as memory is concerned. You know you have certain facts—yet are not able to bring them into consciousness.

"I have forgotten," you will say, and, of course, the statement proves to be true. The fact does not return. If you were to search for the reason, and would use the knowledge you have already learned, you would discover why the information does not come into consciousness.

Reflect back over what you have learned regarding mind and how it operates. You now know that thoughts held by the conscious mind are accepted by the Creative Mind which acts upon them. To say: "I have forgotten!" is, in effect, telling your Creative Mind to do nothing about it. You close the door to your mental storehouse with the definite thought that you have forgotten. Say, instead, "It will come to me in a moment," then you will find it doing so. You have given your Creative Mind a mental instruction to locate the information and bring it into consciousness.

Most people, when they get along in years, accept the thought they have a poor memory. This need not be so, and will not be so, with those who will take seriously that which will be given in this chapter.

As one adds to his years, his interests increase. With a mind flitting from one interest to another, it is quite easy to lose the thread of thought pertaining to any specific interest. As one experiences such tricks of memory, he is quite likely to feel his memory is becoming impaired. He then adds to his mental difficulty by constantly commenting on his bad memory.

Many people talk about their *fading* memory, and while doing so feel they are rapidly joining the class of old people. To such people, let me offer this word of encouragement—*there is no such thing as a fading memory.* Memories do not fade. If you recall to mind a red necktie or hair ribbon you wore when a child, that red has not faded to a pink. If you bring into consciousness the sound of an explosion heard during childhood, that sound hasn't faded down to a slight crackle. No, the red will be as vivid as it originally was; the explosion will be as loud. We might misplace portions of memory, but that which we do recall is as it was when first experienced.

Recently I visited a hotel that I had stayed in five years before. Approaching the desk, the clerk called me by name, mentioning the fact that it must be about five years since he had seen me before and, as I was signing the register, he remarked that he was going to give me the same room I had occupied on my earlier visit. One might show astonishment regarding such a memory, yet that man was doing nothing different from that which any normal individual could do.

A young lady in a phonograph record shop rarely referred to the catalog for numbers of records, although her stock consisted of many thousands of different ones. A customer would ask for a certain selection and this girl, without hesitation, would go direct to the bin where it could be found. She had a good memory, yes, but not better than yours or mine or, to make my statement more acceptable at this time, her memory is no better than yours or mine *might* be.

There are two types of memory training—the *mechanical and the psychological.*

The mechanical means of memory development is through association—association of mental pictures. Usually a series of pictures, either associated with the alphabet or numbers, is memorized. These pictures are considered as mental hooks on which to hang facts to be remembered.

For the sake of illustration, a picture of a beehive might be number 2 in your basic list. The number 2 item on your list of things to be remembered may be a chair you are going to have re-upholstered. So you associate a picture of a damaged chair with a hive of bees. It has been found that the more grotesque you make your mental pictures, the longer will they be remembered. All right, in mentally filing the damaged chair you bring into mind your number 2 picture which is a beehive. All right, why not make your chair a beehive? Where the upholstery is torn, you can see in your mind's eye bees swarming about the seat of the chair and going in and coming out of the opening.

At the time you want to recall the items on your list, when reaching basic picture number 2, you would think of the bees and you would automatically see the damaged chair with the bees.

This method is easy to master and can furnish much fun. When you see men and women doing "memory stunts" by remembering long lists of words, this method is usually used.

But I do not teach this form of memory development. It is habit forming. The more you use it, the more you will have to use it. The one who carries a notebook and writes everything down will reach a point whereby he will quickly lose those facts he fails to make written note of.

I have had my success in the field of memory training by using what I call the psychological method. It is a method whereby you remember because you *know* you have a good memory. And, instead of being habit forming, the more you use the psychological method, the less you will need it.

The Psychological Method. In brief, the psychological method of memory development is not much more than gaining a consciousness of a good memory.

Following are five simple steps to be used in gaining a good memory. If you will think as you read—and apply that which you learn—you will discover that, no matter how good your memory is at present, it will be much better after you have completed this chapter.

STEP ONE. Develop an *awareness* of a good memory. From this moment onward, think of yourself as having a good memory. Hold to the thought, "I have a good memory." For several days, repeat this thought over and over again.

If you have been one of those who have thought of yourself as having a bad memory, it may seem inconsistent to suddenly reverse your thinking and look at yourself as one having a good memory. But, remember, you are as you are because of your former thinking. To change yourself, you will have to change your attitude toward yourself. Each time you say: "I have a good memory!" you are making that condition more of a reality.

To be consistent, hereafter you must refrain from using such thoughts as, "I have a poor memory," "I have forgotten," "I can't remember," etc. To do so will be undoing any good you might otherwise do with the positive thought already suggested. If you wish to recall a bit of information into consciousness, and it doesn't come readily, instead of closing your mental door with an "I have forgotten" thought, say to yourself: "I have a good memory—it will come to me directly." It will not be difficult for you to see the wisdom of this instruction.

Following this step alone would assure you a better memory than you now have. The remaining four steps are given to assist you in making greater strides in the development of a good memory.

STEP TWO. Concentration is the theme of this step. Have you ever tried to listen to a conversation and think of something else at the same time? You probably have, because everyone does so at times. You will later find that you will be unable to recall to mind what you heard, nor what you had been thinking about.

Mental concentration is a great adjunct to memory. It may require a bit of self-discipline at first, especially if you have developed a bad habit of allowing your thoughts to wander.

Perhaps the best place to practice concentration is while reading. It sounds strange to say it, but it is rather common to find people following a printed page with their eyes and be thinking about something else at the same time. And, these same people will wonder what is the matter with them because they have difficulty in remembering what they have read.

As an exercise, take a book which is a bit heavy to read. Read a chapter and then lay it down and try to remember what you have read. If the chapters are long, take a page at a time, trying to remember everything you have read after finishing each page. After carrying on with this exercise for a week or two you will be amazed to find how much more you will get out of your reading.

When listening to a speech, think while you listen, i.e., think about what you are hearing. At the conclusion of the talk try to remember all you heard. You can do this same thing while conversing with others. At the conclusion of the conversation, see if you can recall all that was talked about.

All such exercises will increase your powers of concentration. In other words, you will become *concentration conscious* and will automatically train yourself to focus your thoughts on one thing at a time.

Do you remember faces, but not names? You will be in the minority if you say "no". Do you know *why* you remember faces longer than you do names? It is quite simple. When introduced, the name is seldom pronounced too clearly—and the entire introduction lasts but a second or two. On the other hand, you are looking at the face for the entire length of the conversation. Is it any wonder, then, that it is easier to remember faces than names?

It is quite easy to remember names as well as faces if you will make an effort to do so. When being introduced, mention the name of the person being introduced to you, such as: "I am happy to meet you, Mr. Throckmorton." If the name is an unusual one, comment on it. "That is an unusual name, Mr. Throckmorton. Do you spell it just like it sounds?" Every time you ask a question, add the name, as for instance, "Do you intend to remain in our city long, Mr. Throckmorton?" You see, there are many ways to fix the name in your mind. You might even ask for a card so that you will see the name, thereby taking advantage of the visual as well as oral means of remembering. Writing the name a few times will also help to fix it in your mind.

As a conclusion to Step Two, let me suggest that you begin using your improved memory in making full use of that which you have learned so far in this chapter. In Step One you were told to become *conscious of a good memory;* to think in terms of "I have a *good* memory." In previous chapters you learned that thoughts held in the conscious mind are accepted as patterns by the subconscious or Creative Mind. Now then, when wanting to remember something—instead of permitting negative thoughts to enter your mind, such as: "I hope I won't forget it," say to yourself, "I will remember this."

STEP THREE.   If you were taking up the study of the piano, your instructor would lay out a certain amount of work for you, and show you how to do it. You couldn't play the material, of course, until you exercised sufficiently to cause it to become a part of your Creative Mind. In fact, your teacher would most likely refer to your lesson as *exercises,* because they would be just that.

Mastering Step One and Step Two would give you a good memory, but until the principles contained therein have become a part of your Creative Mind, they will not be of great value to you. Therefore exercises are highly desirable. This step, then, will be the consideration of *memory exercises.*

It is quite certain that many who have read this far will feel that it would have been simple to develop a good memory—*were they a few years younger.* Allow me to say, emphatically, age does not enter into our consideration of memory at all. One can have a poor memory while in the thirties—and he can have a good memory in the eighties. It is not a matter of age but of the use to which you have put your memory.

M. nory exercises will help you to develop that good memory consciousness talked of in Step One. Each time you exercise your memory you add a bit more to your realization that you have a good memory.

Playing with numbers will help to develop your memory because it is not easy to associate numbers as you can objects. When walking along the street, look for big numbers. Numbers on automobile license plates are good. As you pass a car take a quick glance at the plate and attempt to photograph the number in your mind. Turn your eyes from the plate and recall as much of the number as you can. At first you may experience a bit of difficulty in remembering all of the numbers, but as you continue the exercise it will become easier and easier to you. In a short time you will be able to actually *see* the complete number in your mind's eye.

Muscles, not used, will become soft and flabby, regardless of age. Memories, not used, will become sluggish—regardless of age. Memory exercises will not only improve one's memory, but will cause the mind to become more alert. And, they help materially toward developing the powers of concentration.

Memorizing poetry will prove to be a good memory exercise. Begin with short poems and as you fix them in your mind, remember to hold to the thought: "It will be easy for me to learn this." After you find you can easily remember short poems, select long ones, and make them a part of your mental storehouse. There will be found another use for these poems in a later chapter when we consider voice, expression, etc.

Do you do the shopping? Do you make out a list? Practice making your list *mentally*. As you go to the store, instead of wondering whether or not you will remember—*know* that you will. Be happy in the thought that you will remember because you have a good memory.

The most interesting speakers are those who talk freely

and coherently without constantly referring to notes. And, it's easy to do this after you become conscious you have a good memory. So, add such an exercise to your routine. Before conferring with an individual, or talking to a group, *know* that you will recall to mind everything you wish to say.

The exercises suggested do not cover all of them by any means. By using your imagination a bit, you will be able to add many more. The main thing is to exercise that memory of yours—and often.

A fitting close to this step is to urge that as you exercise, do so with a sense of joy. Instead of thinking of your exercises as *work,* which you must do, approach them as you would a fascinating game—and they will be. You will gain so much fun as you find your memory building; instead of resisting the exercises, you will do them every opportunity you have.

STEP FOUR. Develop your powers of observation. Most people see, but do not observe. We see enough so that we will be able to move without colliding with objects—but we do not retain anything regarding that which we do see.

As to whether or not we really observe, right now think of the houses in the block in which you live. How many are there? What colors are they? What do they have in their gardens? Perhaps you have lived in your block for years and have seen the houses daily—yet should you attempt to remember what they look like, you are apt to experience difficulty in doing so.

Perhaps you have an advertising calendar on the wall.

Without looking at it, can you call the name of the advertiser imprinted on it? Not many people will be able to do so.

To show how we see without observing, I will relate an incident which occurred in an office I formerly had in New York City. In conversation with a visitor I asked him if he intended attending a certain exhibition being held in the city. I mentioned the building in which the exhibit was held. It was a large building—a skyscraper, so-called. He asked me where that building was—and when I told him, he admitted with a bit of embarrassment, that he had been passing that building twice daily for years and was not even aware of its existence.

A good way to improve your powers of observation is to change your habit patterns so far as your routes of travel are concerned. If you go to an office or factory each day, instead of going the same way each time, vary it. Go one way—return another. As you do so, see how many interesting things you can see—and later, recall to mind what you did see.

Trips will mean more to you as you develop your powers of observation. You will return with a mind filled with pictures which will keep the trip alive.

You will discover to your pleasure that, as you expand your powers of observation, you will not only be improving your memory, but will gain in many substantial ways. You will become a more interesting conversationalist. And, perhaps, more important than all, you will find a new zest in life.

From this day onward, make observation a part of your

life. Train yourself to *observe* as you *see*. After doing this for one week, you will be startled—yes, actually startled to find how much of life you have been missing.

Boredom is seldom, if ever, experienced by the one who has learned to be observing. If you are with people who are not proving to be interesting, through observation you can really have enjoyment in observing the others; trying to discover why they are as they are. In studying the actions and reactions of people, you learn much. You learn things to do and things not to do. In waiting for a bus or a train, the moments need not drag. Use your eyes. Observe everything within range of your vision. You will discover your thoughts beginning to flow—constructively. Ideas regarding things and people will pour into consciousness.

In gaining the benefit from Step Four, spend a moment each evening in reviewing your observations of the day. You will be surprised to find how interesting this world really is, and how much of this interest has been passing you by unnoticed.

STEP FIVE. In the primary grades in school we learned of our five senses: sight, touch, taste, smell and hearing. So far as memory is concerned, we seldom use more than two of the five senses: sight and sound.

The one with a good memory will use all of his senses—or at least all which apply to the item to be remembered. Through sight you fix all visual properties, size, color, materials, etc. Your touch will tell you much regarding texture, fine or coarse. Taste informs us if an item is sweet or sour or bitter; salty, spicy, etc. Our sense of smell will classify an object as pleasant or repellent. Hearing tells us many things which help us to remember: loud, blatant, raspy, husky, soothing, pleasant, etc.

There is a close relationship between all of these five steps. Any one of them alone will help immeasurably in the development of a good memory, but when you use all five you will gain results which may seem incredible.

CHAPTER FOURTEEN

Conversation—Public Speaking

EVERYONE LIKES TO be a good conversationalist. Many feel that the art of conversation is a trait possessed by few people only. We admire those who can carry on a fascinating conversation. The *good news* is that you, too, may become a good conversationalist, and, if you heed the rules which follow, it will not be as difficult as you might now think.

Invariably, the things we admire in others are those characteristics we do not possess. It is this latter thought which unquestionably holds us back. In our study of *CREATIVE PSYCHOLOGY,* we have learned that thoughts are pictures, and our *mental pictures* are *patterns* which are *accepted* and *acted upon* by our *CREATIVE MINDS.* Therefore, if we hold the thought that we are not good conversationalists, our *CREATIVE MINDS,* without question, will see to it that *we are NOT good conversationalists.* If you hold to the thought *you ARE a good conversationalist, your CREATIVE MIND* will make you one. This means, then, that the first step is to acquire a *CONSCIOUSNESS* that you *ARE* a good conversationalist.

What is a good conversationalist? Merely one possessed with the ability to carry on an interesting conversation. And that of course helps one in both the business and social world. So now if you will do a little work in connection with the following rules, you will surprise yourself to see how much your conversation will improve and how much it will add to your *magnetic personality.*

ACQUIRE A CONVERSATION CONSCIOUSNESS

Think in terms of "I *am* a good conversationalist!" *KNOW* that, when you're with others, you can contribute *your share* toward the conversation, that your thoughts will flow freely and you will be able to express your thoughts easily and interestingly.

This might seem inconsistent to you at first, especially if you have considered yourself as a poor conversationalist up to now; but *motion creates emotion.* The mental pictures you will create of yourself as a good conversationalist will *take root* and *make* you *a good conversationalist.*

ADD TO YOUR STOREHOUSE OF KNOWLEDGE

A good conversationalist must have things to talk about. In this day and age, with information at hand in every direction, there is no *excuse* for any one of us to remain *uninformed.*

1. Read at least one good newspaper *thoroughly* every day so that you will keep posted on current events. A good conversationalist never permits conversation to lag. By keeping up on the topics of the day, you always have a subject on the tip of your tongue to inject—as one subject after another becomes "talked out."

2. Read a few good magazines each month. From them you will gain knowledge of *literature, music, theatre, art, science, etc.*

3. Radio news broadcasts will keep you informed of news which has not yet appeared in the newspapers. Being able to contribute a thought to a conversation which has not yet appeared in the press brands you as *being on your toes.*

4. Television and motion pictures provide good material for the conversationalist. From them you become acquainted with the television and motion picture artists; you may study the technique of acting; you become familiar with various parts of the world; you learn much about photography.

5. Read *advertisements.* There is a definite news value to advertisements. You learn of new things for your home, your table, or your wardrobe; all of which furnishes material for conversation.

ASK QUESTIONS

Many people, when they converse, hesitate to ask questions, fearing they will reveal ignorance. This is *not* the right attitude at all. No one *knows all* about everything; in fact, *no one knows all about ANYTHING*. Even the most learned cannot claim to know *ALL* about the subject of the greatest interest to him. The *more* one learns about anything, the more he finds there is to learn.

It is complimentary to a speaker to ask questions about the subject he is discussing. It shows you are *interested* and, incidentally, you *gain more* from the conversation.

BE A GOOD LISTENER

It is as much of an art to be a good *listener* as it is to be a good *talker*. Listening does not mean merely being silent. It means to show *interest* in what is said, by *looking at the speaker* instead of permitting your gaze to wander about.

ADD VARIETY TO THE CONVERSATION

Unless a group is assembled for the purpose of discussing a specific subject, it is well to add variety to a conversation. Before any one topic reaches the state of becoming boring, change to another one. Be observing, and you can tell by the expression on the faces whether or not a subject is *really* interesting.

DO NOT "HOG" THE CONVERSATION

A conversation is *not* a monologue. It is an exchange of ideas and thoughts. Just as it is *desirable* for you to do your part in contributing to a conversation, so too is it necessary to give others an opportunity to add their share.

LEARN BY DOING

Practice makes perfect. Each time you learn a new fact, talk about it. Explain it to someone. This gives you experience in the art of conversation.

PRACTICE VOICE EXPRESSION

A speaking voice can be *musical,* just as a singing voice. Practice voice expression. Give *life* to words! It is a good exercise to read aloud, giving expression to every word. Take a chapter from the book you are reading, and see how well you can express it—give thought to every word you utter. You will be pleasantly surprised to discover how your speaking voice will improve.

GIVE WARMTH TO YOUR VOICE

When you talk to people, hold friendly feelings toward them, then there will be warmth in your voice, and it will cause these people to *like* you.

1, 2, 3 METHOD OF PUBLIC SPEAKING

Do you remember how jittery you were the last time you attended club meeting? The president was selecting the member who would give the talk at the next session. You crouched a bit low in your chair—making yourself less conspicuous—while your heart was gaining momentum as you thought: "Gracious, suppose he would call on me!"

You did heave a sigh of relief when another name was mentioned and, as your heart returned to normalcy, you became a bit more talkative to those around you as you gave vent to the feelings you had suppressed during the anxious moments.

You were unhappy that night. You did not sleep very well. You tossed from one side of the bed to the other as you tried to visualize yourself at the speaker's table and, with perfect poise, a well modulated voice, and an easy flow of expressive words, you held the rapt attention of your listeners.

"Why can't I do that?" you ask yourself over and over again, as you recall how panicky you get when the speaker is being selected—and *YOU* might be called. Then you remember the many things you have read and heard about *public speaking*. You had heard Mrs. Ipswitch tell of the time her husband gave a talk at the Sales Manager's Club. He stayed up three nights until well after midnight preparing his speech. The members of the family had to sit through at least a dozen or more rehearsals, and the night before the big event the neighbors were called in for the final "dress" rehearsal. And, with the perfection Mr. Ipswitch felt he had obtained, everything went black before him as he started his talk to the Club.

You think about the young attorney Jones, who was elected to the State Assembly, and who spent countless hours in his barn giving speeches to imaginary audiences.

Then you mentally review the books you have read on Public Speaking. You must walk to the platform *just so;*

you must acquire a *faultless* stance. Your recognition of the Chair, greeting to the audience, type of illustrative stories told, must be in keeping with the decorum of such meetings.

"No, no, no!" you say to yourself. "Public speaking is not for me. One cannot *learn it*. One has to be a *born speaker*," you reason, and so you let it go at that.

Phooey! Stuff and Rubbish!!!

You have been speaking in public ever since you learned to talk. Every time you say a word to another person, you are speaking in public. That which you have been fearing are imaginary mountains made out of molehills.

You will not have to spend months, perhaps years, in practice to enable you to talk from a platform. If, right now, you'll pause a moment, get yourself thoroughly relaxed, and make up your mind that you will read the rest of this chapter slowly, carefully, and thoughtfully, you will be able to step up to the platform tomorrow and give a talk—and it will be a *good* one.

I have lectured to audiences in every city in the United States over 50,000 population, and I have never taken a speaking lesson in my life. I have a file filled with flattering letters from clubs, business and social organizations and groups of all kinds, commending me for the talks.

At one time, I made an analysis of a few of my own talks to learn what method I had unknowingly discovered which made it so simple for me to talk from the platform. I talk from the briefest outline of notes and with very little advance preparation. On the radio I'm one of the few allowed to *ad lib* from notes instead of from carefully—and fully—prepared scripts. Right now you are thinking that I am one of the extravert types who find it natural to appear before large groups, but you're wrong—decidedly so. Up to the age of thirty I was the type of a timid soul which must have inspired Webster when he created Casper Milquetoast.

My study of the format of my talks revealed that, without consciously doing so, I had appropriated some of the psychological principles I had learned, and which I had built into my lectures.

It was found that the most logical and psychological way of laying out a lecture is on the basis of three's. Three main parts—and each part subdivided into three phases. The conclusions reached seemed too simple. I felt there must be a catch somewhere, so I decided I would experiment with this "1, 2, 3 Method" to learn if it did have merit, and if others would find the *same* ease in talking as the *one-time* timid me was able to do.

In San Francisco, where I have conducted many classes on *CREATIVE PSYCHOLOGY*, I told one of my groups of adults I was going to make public speakers of them—and proceeded to outline the 1, 2, 3 Method of Public Speaking. The results were surprisingly good. Within a week, all of them were able to stand on the platform and talk from notes—*not* prepared speeches. One woman, who had formerly been so timid she would hesitate to answer a question in class, made a splendid talk—and later accepted a speaking engagement from a club.

THE 1, 2, 3 METHOD. Recall to mind a few of the last lectures you heard. How many things can you remember from each talk? You will be able to recall *three* things told by the speakers—*seldom more.* If the speaker tried to cover too many topics during his address, your mind, in trying to retain *all* of them, becomes confused and you might not even remember as many as three things. But it has been learned that the mind can and *will* retain *three different thoughts* given in one talk. All right! Now you have learned an important principle. *Do NOT attempt to cover MORE than THREE THOUGHTS in any ONE LECTURE.*

At this point, it will be well to show you how easy it is to cover these three thoughts without writing them down or without laboriously memorizing them.

You have no difficulty in remembering a story, do you? You can go to a movie and later describe, in considerable detail, a picture which might have taken 1½ to 2 hours to see, can't you? The reason for this is easy to understand. There has been a continuity of thought. All right! Just think of the three parts of your talk as three stories. Simple, isn't it? And as you tell these stories, they will make better listening, because you will be giving them naturally —and not in the *stiff style* you would use if you were to write them down beforehand.

When you're out with friends and stories are told, you will often jot down just a "key thought" to enable you to recall to mind the real choice stories. Well, that is all you have to do in connection with the three stories you will tell *when you are giving a talk.* Just jot down the *key thought,* a few words which will bring the stories freshly to your mind.

Now then, I will give you a surefire way of telling your three stories so they will be impressed on the minds of your listeners. This, too, involves the rule of three.

A colored parson of the south, one noted for his oratory, was asked for his formula of a successful sermon. His reply was as fascinating as it was logical. "First I tell them what I'm going to tell them. Then I tell them what I'm telling them. Then I tell them what I told them." Isn't this thought sound? Certainly. All right, use it in connection with your three points. Divide each story into three parts: the *LEAD,* the *STORY,* and the *CLIMAX.*

Here you have the 1, 2, 3 Method of Public Speaking. You can write the notes for an entire talk on a small filing card; one which you can hold in the palm of your hand. You will have three principle *key thoughts* representing the three major points (or stories) of your talk. Under each *key thought,* you may—if you desire—add sub-notes covering the three parts of your story. A total of nine brief notes will cover an entire talk.

Examples

It might prove helpful if a few illustrations are given covering talks of various kinds.

Suppose you were preparing a talk for the local Parent Teacher's Association. You, having had considerable experience with children, are asked to talk on Child Psychology. How would you break that subject down in three parts?

Naturally, the subject is such a large one it would be easily possible to use a dozen or more phases, but *not you.* You would rather take *three* points, and have them remembered by your listeners, than several points more and *not having anything* stick. How about: 1. *Pre-natal influences,* 2. *Post-natal training,* and 3. *Adolescence?* You see? A big subject broken down into three interesting parts.

The High Hat Study Club might ask you to tell the members something about your recent trip into Mexico. "Gosh, there's a toughy," the unaccustomed speaker would say. But the "One, Two, Three-er" would nonchalantly take a pencil, write the numbers 1, 2, 3, and, with but a moment's meditation, write after the number such thoughts as: 1. *The Trip,* 2. *Comparative Geography,* and 3. *The People.* You need no more illustrations. You are ahead of me.

QUESTIONS

Yes, at this moment there may be a few questions in your mind—but they are easily answered.

HOW LONG SHALL I TALK?   This is a good question. After twenty minutes, the listeners begin looking at their watches. After thirty minutes, they shake their watches to make sure they are running. *Play* safe and do not talk more than 25 minutes. Remember, it is better to give 'em a bit less than they want, than to have them think: "Thank heaven that is over." Do not give several attempted endings by saying: "And in conclusion," etc. Cover your subject, then cut. If you come to an unexpected end the listeners will be a bit disappointed. They will wish they had more. That is an ideal condition. It is *your VICTORY!*

HOW LOUD SHOULD I TALK?   If you were in a hall with just one person, and you were at one end of the room and he at the other, you would automatically raise your voice enough so that he could hear it clearly, wouldn't you? That gives you the answer to your question. Imagine you are talking to someone in the back row and your voice will be just right.

HOW SHALL I STAND? MOVE? GESTURE?   Don't try to imitate any speaker. Develop your own personality. Do the things which are natural to you. Gesture only when you feel inclined to do so *naturally.*

HOW CAN I OVERCOME MY TIMIDITY?   If you have given sufficient thought to Chapters Seven and Eleven, you will not ask this question; but right here I can give you a point of great value in connection with public speaking. Let me ask you a question. In a crowd, is there a single person whom you would hesitate to talk to individually? No? Well, remember, the *INTELLIGENCE* of an *AUDIENCE* is *NOT MULTIPLIED* by the number of people present. It is no greater than the intelligence of one person. And since there is no one person you would hesitate to talk to individually, there's no reason at all why you should fear to talk to a group of them.

There's just one more thought I want to leave with you, and then you will be all ready to throw your hat in the ring as a *Public Speaker.*

Instead of fearing your audience, *love it.* If you have affection in your heart for those who have come to hear you, there will be warmth in your voice, and as you project your personality down through your audience, you will thrill as you sense the affection radiating back to you.

And, to your *first appearance*—here is my sustained *applause!*

CHAPTER FIFTEEN

How to Make Good in the Field of Salesmanship

SALESMANSHIP IS ONE of the most thrilling occupations on earth—if—if one approaches the work as a profession instead of a job.

It may seem like an exaggeration to say that the fundamentals of salesmanship can be given in one chapter, yet, I have the courage to state that with what you have learned so far in this book, and with that which will be contained in this chapter, a person who has never had any sales training at all can make good in the field of selling—and those already in the work will be able to materially increase their earnings.

Perhaps it would be well to open with the statement that a salesman never sells anything but himself—the prospect *buys*. This being true we could add that the function of a salesman is to create a desire on the part of the prospect to buy.

Another truth, seldom recognized by those engaged in selling is that, in a majority of cases, the prospect wants that which you are selling. If he doesn't buy, it is because he has been unable to sell himself on buying, which brings up the point that *the real selling is done on the part of the prospect—and not the salesman.*

It might sound a bit strange to say that the reason why many people fail to make good salesmen is because they try to sell their product; yet it is true. No matter how good your product might be, your prospect will not buy until he can sell himself on doing so. This leads us to one of the basic principles in selling. *Instead of spending time in talking about how good your product is, dwell on how good your product will make your prospect.*

Salesmanship might be symbolized with a triangle. One point being the product, another the prospect, and the third point—the sale. In other words, a salesman functions by bringing the product (or service) and the prospect together in a manner resulting in a sale.

To back up the statement first made to the effect that salesmanship is one of the most thrilling professions, let us think of the components which make up a top notch salesman. In this analysis we are thinking of the type of man who takes the work just as seriously as the doctor, lawyer or architect takes his profession.

A good salesman is a psychologist. He must understand the motives which influence men. He should be able to understand his prospect so that he may present his arguments in a manner which will appeal to that particular type of individual.

A good salesman is a diplomat. When the prospect disagrees, the salesman must be able to tactfully show the prospect where he is wrong without offending.

A good salesman must be a business man. In many cases he will have the opportunity to counsel with his prospects, thereby proving of greater worth, and, of course, producing more business for himself and his firm.

A good salesman must have a working knowledge of merchandising and advertising. He will understand the strategy of the advertising and merchandising campaigns and will be able to capitalize upon this knowledge in connection with his work in selling.

A good salesman is resourceful. Naturally prospects will not say "yes" immediately, and in many cases will blurt out with a thunderous "NO!" The resourceful salesman is the one who will invent ways and means of causing a prospect to reverse his decision and act in the affirmative.

A good salesman is analytical. He must be able to analyze his product for its most dominant sales points. He must be able to analyze the products of his competitors, so that he may build his arguments to offset the claims of competition. He must be able to analyze statistics and from them gain data which will prove helpful to him.

A good salesman has a well developed imagination. He can see in his mind's eye his prospect using and being benefited by his product so clearly, that it will be simple for him to work out ways and means of making such a mental picture a reality.

A good salesman is always popular. His knowledge of

psychology, his ability to understand and get along with people, makes him conspicuous in any gathering.

The good salesman is a fascinating conversationalist. The variety of contacts he is daily making, and the numerous conversations he is hearing and partaking in, gives him an evergrowing storehouse of conversational material.

The good salesman is a man of affairs. The salesman who makes his work a profession is in the higher brackets so far as income is concerned. Most employes are considered an expense to the firm. This is not true with a salesman. He is an asset—a producer. Salaries up to $25,000 per year, and even higher, are not uncommon in the field of selling. Salesmen are usually compensated on a basis of business produced, which means that the "sky is the limit" so far as earnings are concerned. The more skill, resourcefulness and enthusiasm you put into your work, the greater will be your compensation.

A good salesman is in a far better position than the owner of a retail store. In reality, the retailer is merely a salesman selling on a percentage basis, but think of the risk involved. He has many expenses which are fixed, regardless of the amount of business he might do, such as rent, light, heat, etc. Then, of course, he has a big investment in merchandise, so he must certainly figure the interest this money would earn, and charge this lost interest to overhead expenses. The salesman has no expenses and no overhead, except his personal living expenses which he would have with any kind of a job.

Perhaps, when we are in contact with a live-wire salesman and observe his air of self-confidence and his thorough satisfaction with life, our envy is such we doubt if we could ever reach such a point ourselves.

You are now learning you do not need to envy the big producer, because you're on the road toward being one yourself. You doubt this? All right, answer the simple question: "Why?" You'll begin to fumble around for a reply, and the longer you fumble, the more difficult it will be to offer a plausible answer, because there will be none. You cannot base the difference on physical characteristics, because you have seen outstanding salesmen who were weaklings from the standpoint of physique. You might consider education as the principal difference, yet you can think of many sales people who are making big money and yet have less education than you have. As you grope around in an attempt to justify the difference between the high ranking salesman and the one who just gets by, you are forced to the conclusion that the real reason for the go-getter's success is that he *knows* he can sell. As the title of this book suggests, he thinks in terms of "I Can!"

Here is a truth seldom thought of in connection with salesmanship. No salesman ever sells anything. Does this sound inconsistent with what you have been reading so far? *A prospect buys.* All a salesman does is to create a desire on the part of the prospect to buy that which you have to offer. And, it may sound strange to say that in a majority of cases the prospect wants that which you have to offer. "Then," you might ask, "why doesn't he buy?" The reason is that the real selling job is on the part of the prospect—he must sell himself. If he doesn't buy, it is

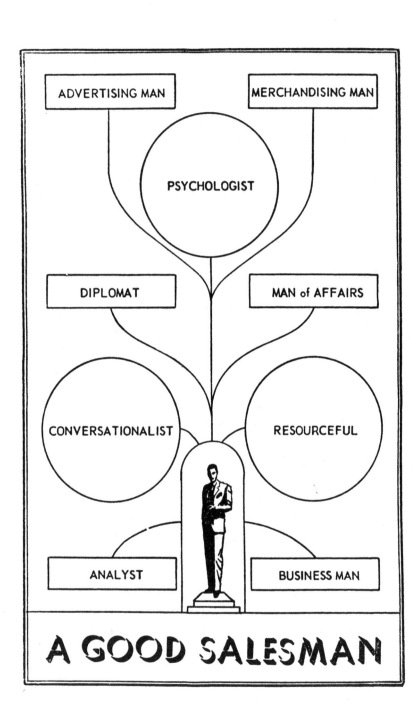

because he has not been able to sell himself. This being true, the successful salesman thinks of the many reasons why the prospect should buy, thereby helping him to sell himself. It is this type of reasoning which will give you a glimpse into the joys and thrills you will get once you enter the field of selling from the psychological viewpoint

Since, in this book, you have learned much regarding the mind and how it operates, you will know how to encourage the prospect to sell himself. You know the impulses which influence *your* actions; you will know those which will influence action on the part of the prospect. . . .

Discouragement will be unknown to you because every contact you have with a prospect offers fascinating opportunities for further learning. If you make the sale, you will have learned things which will help toward future sales. If you do not land the order your enthusiasm and interest in your work will cause you to study the case to discover why you did not make the sale; thereby making a stepping stone of that which might otherwise have been considered a failure.

You will be in a position to control your own earnings. If you are averaging one sale out of four interviews, and you are having, let us say, twelve interviews each day, this will mean three sales each day. If, through the use of greater efficiency in your work, you can have 16 interviews in a day, according to the law of averages, you would then make four sales each day, thereby increasing your sales by one-third. After you are making as many interviews per day as your well-calculated time will permit, then, through the use of more applied psychology, you might be able to change your average of sales from one out of four, to one out of three interviews. This adds another substantial sum to your income.

THE PRODUCT

A salesman is looked upon as an authority on the product or service he is selling. If he sells a machine, for example, he is expected to be in a position to intelligently answer all questions pertaining to that machine; what it will do and how it does it; its economy, durability, dependability, etc. If it is a service he is selling, he must be able to present logical arguments as to why the prospect should use it.

There is one basic fundamental in salesmanship which should be stressed. *A salesman must be sold on the product or service he is selling.* Unless you are so thoroughly sold on your product that you would do what you might expect your prospect to do—there is little hope of climbing very high in selling that product. Satisfied customers are a great asset to a salesman. You gain business from them and through them.

It may, at first, sound strange to say this, but, in reality, your prospect does not buy your product at all—he buys the product of the product. A man does not buy an automobile—he buys transportation. He does not buy advertising—he buys increased business. When purchasing medicine, it is health he is after. In saving money, one is not doing so merely for the fine engravings found on the currency—but for what the money represents: security, comfort, travel, education, etc. A salesman, for example, was making but little progress selling oil burners. He knew his product well and could give a good talk on the principles of combustion involved in his burner. After he began selling the product of the product—a recreation room instead of space with a coal bin and ash barrels—his sales began to climb.

How much should a salesman know about his product? Although he is selling the product of the product, he should know much about the product and its manufacture, such as:

1. Integrity of those behind the product.

2. The factory producing the product.

3. Materials and construction.

4. Be familiar with the use of the product.

5. Understand costs; production, operation, maintenance, etc.

6. The dominant appeal.

Although there are many arguments in favor of nearly any product, there is usually one outstanding, or dominant, appeal. Build on the dominant and make all other arguments subordinate to it. In transportation, for example, speed is the dominant appeal for airplanes; comfort for trains, and economy for buses. When selecting your dominant appeal, you will take that feature which is special and cannot be said by your competitor. Playing up this dominant will make it difficult for your competitor to undermine you, should you not be able to close the order on your first interview.

THE MARKET

Your market means your prospects, the people or firms who can buy and be benefited by that which you have to offer.

The answers to the following questions will give you a picture of your market.

1. Who are your prospects?

2. Where are your prospects?

3. What do they buy?

4. How do they buy?

5. Where do they buy?

6. When do they buy?

A salesman's accomplishments depend largely on his efficiency. Seeing the right prospect at the right time is one the keys to his success. Giving sufficient consideration to the above questions will add much to one's effectiveness.

There are two other questions regarding the market which should always be present in the mind of the professional salesman:

1. Can new markets be created?

2. Can new uses be found?

Creating new markets and new uses automatically expands the number of sales possibilities.

THE INTERVIEW

A sales interview should be organized. One, to be successful, approaches the prospect with a well organized plan. There are four distinct phases to a sales interview:

1. The greeting.

2. The need.

3. The solution.

4. How to obtain.

The greeting. In many cases the order is won or lost during the first moment or two of the interview. The prospect will form a quick impression of you as soon as you enter his presence; therefore you must prepare yourself so as to create a good first impression.

"Fear attracts that which is feared," is psychologically true, and particularly so as far as salesmanship is concerned. If you fear talking to a prospect, your attitude reflects that fear. You will enter his home or office with an attitude almost apologetic. Your prospect senses your uneasiness and gives you quick relief by terminating the interview in an instant.

Approach your prospect with poise and self-assurance. A prospect feels just as uncomfortable in the presence of a timid, nervous individual as such a person feels in the presence of the prospect. When you are at ease, the prospect is more inclined to be at ease.

In greeting our prospect, instead of using the moth-eaten weather forecast opening, "break the ice" with a compliment. "I am honored to meet the man responsible for this great institution," will get more orders than, "It's certainly a fine day, isn't it?"

The Need. A prospect is never interested in a product or service unless he has need for it. Therefore to spend your time in first telling how good your product is will be a waste of time. Build your arguments around the need for your product—and be diplomatic in doing so. A prospect resents having an outsider tell him about his business and how to run it. A discussion regarding the general need for such products will avoid "stepping on the toes" of the prospect.

The Solution. After your prospect agrees with you regarding the need for a certain product or service, then you have reached the point of discussing the object of your meeting. And present your product from your prospect's point of view. Devote your presentation to those points which will apply directly to the prospect and prove to be of greatest benefit to him. Without actually saying so, you can present your argument so effectively, the prospect will almost feel the equipment was especially designed for him.

How to Obtain the Product. It is not until you have established the need for your product, and convinced your prospect that your product will fill such a need, that he is interested at all in where and how to get that which you offer.

After you are sure in your own mind that the prospect has mentally accepted your product, then you can begin talking about details as to terms and delivery.

THE PROSPECT SELLS HIMSELF

You have already learned that the prospect sells himself. Therefore, the salesman, instead of devoting most of his time in telling the prospect how good his product is—as mentioned elsewhere—will stress the reasons regarding how good the product will make the prospect.

Following are a few questions which the prospect mus. answer to his satisfaction before he will be able to sel. himself.

Can I Afford the Item? It will be the job of the salesman to put reasons in the mind of the prospect which will convince him he cannot afford to be *without* the product.

Is It Good Business to Buy That Which Is Offered? Here the salesman will prove that it is good business. The prospect will be shown how the product adds to his comfort, efficiency, income, standing—or any other arguments which might apply to that which is presented.

Will I Be Thought Extravagant? To the contrary, he will be made to feel progressive. He will be looked up to as one who keeps up with the times; a leader among men. It is true that to appear successful is frequently the first step toward being successful. This fact will be emphasized to the prospect.

Is Now a Good Time to Buy?   Procrastination is one of the greatest resistances encountered by the salesman. The prospect might agree he likes the product—and that he will buy it—eventually. Knowing that the thought of putting it off might be lurking in the mind of the prospect, the salesman will make it obvious that now is the right time to buy. Prices going up, quantity on hand is diminishing, losing benefits to be gained by possessing product—are just a few of the many possible arguments which can be used.

Perhaps There Are Other Brands Better Than the One Being Considered.   Knocking competitors is a great mistake and seldom helps in any way. Instead it focuses attention on the competitor and often makes the prospect wonder why the salesman is afraid of his competition. The intelligent salesman backs his arguments with sufficient proof to cause the prospect to feel that his product leads the field. Paying compliments to your competitors' product, usually raises your own in the estimation of the prospect. They realize you are sure of yourself, otherwise you could not be so generous with praise toward those in the same field.

An excellent suggestion to offer at this time is: Recall to mind the reasons why you didn't buy some of the things which were offered to you. Those same reasons might be holding your prospect back. And, remember this: The reasons for not purchasing as given by a prospect are not often the real reasons. If he can use and be benefited by that which you have to offer, and he does not buy it, it indicates that he has been unable to sell himself on buying. It will, therefore, be necessary for you to anticipate why he has not sold himself and then provide arguments which will assist him in doing so.

CHAPTER SIXTEEN

How to Get a Better Job

THE DISTINGUISHED Dr. Russell Conwell, in his world famous book, "Acres of Diamonds," proved quite conclusively that many of us are looking elsewhere for that which we have right at hand. His theories can apply to jobs as well as anything else. Perhaps a little story will explain what I am leading up to:

Robert Brown (we'll call him) was disgruntled with his job—very much so. His work was unpleasant, his income was small; those he worked with were snobbish and uncooperative; his boss was indeed unfair. These were a few of the reasons Bob gave when asking me to help him find a better job.

I questioned Bob at length regarding his job. "Would you be happy with it, if all of those conditions were changed?" I queried.

"Well, yes, I guess so," replied Bob, after reflecting a moment. "But," he added, "how can those conditions be changed? It has been like that for the three years I have worked there."

"Why, the methods we use are old-fashioned. I could take that department and show them how to do more and better work in less time and with less labor," Bob stated, after I had succeeded in getting him in a talkative mood. He then spent ten minutes in explaining to me how the methods of manufacture used by the company for which he works could be greatly improved.

"Have you explained your ideas to the company?" I asked offhandedly.

"Aw, what's the use?" he retorted, almost caustically. "What thanks would they give me?" he continued.

After discussing Bob's job for a half hour or so, I sought a little information regarding those with whom he works.

"How many of your associates do you like?" I fired as a first question in this direction.

"I don't like any of them," he asserted with definiteness, "and," he continued, "why should I?"

Since Bob Brown had come to me for assistance, I extracted a promise from him. I told him I would help him get another job if he still wanted it after having tested a formula I would give him regarding the job he did have. Reluctantly, he promised.

The attitude his associates had toward him was a reflection of the attitude he had toward them. It is impossible to hide your feelings. If you dislike people, people will dislike you. I suggested to Bob, therefore, that his first step was to like those with whom he worked; to greet them with a friendly word and smile, and to cooperate with them each time an opportunity would present itself.

The next thing Bob should do would be to seek an audience with his boss and explain in detail the methods he had conceived for making the work in his department more efficient.

Not to carry this illustration too far, permit me to tell you what happened. Bob soon became very popular with those in his department, and after explaining his theories to his superior, he was given the position of foreman with full authority to put his ideas into operation. And, of course, he was granted a very liberal increase in salary. Does he want to change his job? You know the answer to that question. He feels he has one of the best jobs in the city and with the finest company in the country.

The desire to improve one's self is admirable and it is one which should be possessed by everyone. To wish for a better job indicates a progressive spirit. However, in looking for a better job, start first by carefully considering the job you're in at present. What are your chances for promotion, if you make a study of the job ahead of you? Remember, it is far better to grow in the job in which you now find yourself than it is to get a new job with a different company. To be advanced with your present company means that you are established with those in power. To change to another company means you are starting with people who do not know you as an employe—and you have no assurance they will like you after you make the new connection.

I had lunch one day with the head of a chain of retail stores. "In opening new stores, Ben," he remarked candidly, "one of my greatest problems is to find men qualified to manage them." He told me about the hundreds of employes he has, but how few of them show sufficient interest to study and prepare for the job ahead of them.

If you are not fully satisfied with your job as is, ask yourself a few of the following questions to learn whether or not that better job you're after might not be within your grasp—and without leaving your present company.

1. Do you like the company for which you work?

2. Do you like the merchandise made or sold by the company?

3. Do you like the management of the company?

4. Do you get along well with those with whom you work?

5. Are you always punctual?

6. Do you enjoy the work you are doing? If not, why?

7. Do you constantly strive to improve your work?

8. Are you frequently off on sick leave?

9. Does your salary or wages enable you to live comfortably?

10. Would you like to leave the firm for which you work?

A brief discussion of the questions asked should help one in determining whether or not the better job may be had with your present employer or if it might be advisable to seek a change.

Do You Like the Company for Which You Work? To work for a company you do not like and be happy, presents a next to impossible situation.

Without knowing to whom this statement might apply, I can safely say that in many cases our dislike for a company is a reflection of our attitude toward it. A guilty conscience will often make us feel unfriendly toward our employers. Those who are not doing their best, who are disloyal, who fail to put in a full day's work, are quite apt to hold a wrong feeling toward the firm and its management. Psychologically, our resentment toward the firm is an unconscious feeling we hold toward ourselves.

To resolve to give your employer the best you have is a sure way of gaining a friendly feeling toward him and the company.

There are those who take the attitude: "What does the boss care for me? Why should I put myself out for him?" Of course this is a very narrow-minded view to take. Since you will be unable to recall the names of anyone who has climbed to great heights with such an attitude, you will quickly conclude that one of the first steps in gaining promotion with the company in which you are now employed is to learn to genuinely like the company.

Do You Like the Merchandise Made or Sold by the Company? A man will never make great progress with any company unless he can be genuinely enthusiastic over the product of that company. If you have disliked the firm you are with, it will be easy to understand why you might not like the product made or sold by it. As pointed out in the preceding pages, if you can learn to like the company, it is quite likely your feeling toward the product will be enhanced.

If you cannot sincerely like the product you are associated with, if you feel the public is being taken advantage of, then you would be fully justified in seeking a change with a company whose product you accept enthusiastically. There are not many companies, however, which are willfully trying to put something over on the public. Most products have a right to existence, and one will usually find that the moment he begins taking a genuine interest in the company his feeling toward the product will grow.

Do You Like the Management of the Company? It is common for certain employes to feel that the management is partial to some and impartial to others. This is true in a few remote cases—but fortunately such employers are definitely in the minority. A man, to become a leader, must display the qualities of leadership; and not treating all employes fairly indicates a definite lack of leadership.

If you do not like the management of the company, try to discover why. Perhaps looking within will give you the correct answer.

For a period of time, try showing respect for the man who directs the company. Learn to like him and see how many things you can do to please him. The first thing you know, you will be bragging about the wonderful boss you have.

Do You Get Along Well with Those with Whom You

Work?   As you learned in previous chapters, to have people like you, you must like people.

Jealousy and envy are too often reasons why we do not get along with those with whom we work. If an employe gets a break, it is quite easy to feel he is a favorite of the boss. Usually such breaks are deserved and, instead of envying those who get the breaks, it is easy to so conduct yourself the breaks will be coming to you, too.

I once witnessed a situation where an employe refused to do a job which would normally be done by another. "That's not my job. I'm not getting paid for doing that," he protested bitterly. Another employe overhearing the conversation said, "Let me do it, I can find the time." Due to business conditions the foreman had to reduce the size of his staff. Which one of these two employes remained? The answer is obvious.

It is easy to have your associates like you, but you must first like them.

Are You Always Punctual?   Ordinarily, the employe who is always on the dot to stop at the moment of closing time, is not always on the dot in checking in in the mornings.

On one occasion I was the guest of an executive of a large publishing company.

"Come with me, Ben," he suggested, "and I will show you how we can learn the interest—or lack of it—our employes have in their work." It was a few moments before quitting time, and the chief took me to a point of vantage where we could overlook the stenographic department—a large room where at least 50 girls were employed. We could not be observed from where we were stationed.

The quitting bell rang at five o'clock, and, almost like a great machine coming to a stop, all activity ceased—with but few exceptions. Most girls stopped their typing with partially finished letters in the machine, closed their desks, and were off to the cloak room. There were a few girls, however, who spent an extra moment in finishing the page in the typewriter and seeing to it that everything in their desks was properly placed so as to be ready for quick starting in the morning.

This employer was not interested in the few minutes of time he got from these conscientious employes; he was impressed with the serious manner in which they took their work. And, it was those girls who were always considered for better jobs when promotions were in order.

Do You Enjoy the Work You Are Doing? The average person exerts more energy on his days off than he does at work—and with less fatigue. A man can work in his hobby shop from early morning to late at night and will have to be literally dragged away from there for meals and retiring at night. He enjoys doing things in his hobby shop because to him it is fun—not work.

The moment you learn to enjoy your work, you will find you will do better work and your time will pass much more quickly. Instead of watching the clock in hopes the time will pass, you will jealously guard every moment, trying to accomplish the most during the time you have. You can learn to enjoy any work, so long as you have to do it.

A woman once told me of an experience which was indeed interesting. She felt quite sorry for herself because it was necessary for her to scrub the floors in her kitchen and bathroom.

One night she went to a picture show and the principal movie was a marine story. In one of the scenes, the sailors were busily engaged scrubbing the decks. While doing so, instead of feeling sorry for themselves, they were all singing a happy marine song, and actually guiding their movements by the rhythm of the music.

On the following Saturday when it was time to "swab her own decks," she imagined herself a sailor on the briny deep and as she scrubbed the linoleum, she sang, just as the sailors had done.

"It took me no time at all to wash my floors," she exclaimed, "and I was not a bit tired after I finished."

Learn to enjoy your work and note how much more refreshed you will be at the end of the day—not saying anything about an improved disposition. There is far less friction in the home of the person who gets fun from his work.

Do You Constantly Strive to Improve Your Work?   One evening I visited the home of a friend and found him bent over a drafting board making some sketches. In answer to my question as to what he was doing, he told me that he had an idea for improving the product on which he was working in a local factory. His boss knew nothing of the idea; this man was doing it because of his interest in his work. I happen to know that this chap has had four increases in salary in the three years he has been in his present job.

Some people might question the wisdom of spending spare time in the interest of an employer, but it consistently pays off. If you might doubt this, ask yourself a question: "What would be my attitude toward an employe who was always spending his time in my interest?" Wouldn't you want to keep such an employe happy? I think so.

To those of you who are always trying to improve your work, there is no necessity of asking you the question as to whether or not you enjoy your work. You most certainly do.

Are You Frequently Off on Sick Leave? A survey once made showed there was nearly three times as much sickness among employes who did not enjoy their work than among those who did. And, to any psychologist, this is not a bit surprising.

Today we hear much of psychosomatic illness; illness which originates in mind and through the emotions. Do you know why there is more illness among those who dislike their work than among those who do not? Your subconscious, or Creative Mind, has reasoning faculties independent of your conscious mind. If you dislike your work, an illness will give you a valid reason for being away from it. So, your faithful Creative Mind brings on illness giving you a plausible reason to leave your work. The reverse, of course, is true. When you thoroughly enjoy your work, you do not want to be away from it any more than you have to. Therefore, your Creative Mind will work toward keeping you on top, physically.

School children who dislike school will be ill far more than those who enjoy their time in the classroom. The best way to treat frequent illness of the child is to find ways and means of getting him to thoroughly enjoy his classwork.

A young lady who had averaged three sick spells each month was about to be replaced on account of it. In questioning her about her work it was found that she literally detested the foreman of her department. It was suggested that she use the compliment idea as explained elsewhere in this book, and intentionally make a friend of this man. At first she shied from the idea, but her situation was such a difficult one, she agreed to try. She did win him over to a point where they really liked each other. What happened? Now this woman is rarely away on account of illness, and is extremely happy in her work.

If you are frequently ill, perhaps by changing your attitude toward your firm and its employes, you may find your health improving.

Does Your Salary or Wages Enable You to Live Comfortably? If your answer to this question is "no," a light might be dawning for you as you read this chapter. This is hard for some to believe, but, in most cases, the money we acquire is based on the belief we have in ourselves. The one with success consciousness will, if he feels the need of more money, contrive ways and means of earning more. It is my belief that it is hard to hold down the man who really believes in himself. Following through on the thoughts outlined in this chapter will act as fuel in spurring on the one who sincerely wants to make progress in his work.

Would You Like to Leave the Firm for Which You Work? If, after having carefully contemplated the foregoing questions and your answers to them, you still feel you would better yourself by making a change, then thoughtfully consider that which follows.

Locating a New Job

Sometimes it is easier to get a job than to get out of it. If you are seeking a new job, do so in a manner which will assure you a permanent job, a profitable job, a happy job. Here are a few simple steps which will prove magical in helping you to locate just the job you want.

1. *What kind of a job do you want?* It is unfortunate, but true, that many people, in seeking employment, are guided almost entirely by compensation. Unless you can become enthusiastic over a company and its product, you are not destined to climb to great heights in that field.

In deciding on the work you want, you might use the questions already asked in this chapter as a yardstick. Picking the right company, with the right product, will prove most profitable.

2. *Have you the necessary training for the job?* In this day and age, it is not necessary for anyone to lack sufficient knowledge for a job higher up. With our libraries, university extension courses, home study programs, trade papers, magazines, newspapers, radio, television, etc., there is little excuse for anyone to be deprived of knowledge.

In seeking a job in a new field, it is better to take time in preparing for it, than to take a job and not be able to handle it properly.

How to Get a New Job

Letters of application still prove to be the most effective way of getting a job. Remember, however, that there are letters and letters.

Most letters of application are written entirely around the selfish thought of wanting a job for financial reasons. Make your letter a "you" letter instead of a "me" letter. Tell the prospect what you have to offer which will make his business better—and he will be interested.

When operating an advertising agency in New York, and during the dark days of the 1929 depression, the streets were filled with men and women seeking jobs. Their solicitations were nearly all alike. They would give you a sorrowful tale as to their need for a job; but rarely would you find one seeking employment on the basis of what he could give to an employer.

An advertising man from the Pacific Northwest picked out my firm as one he would like to work for. He did not write telling of his financial circumstances. Instead he filled several pages with ideas as to what he could do to increase my business. And he did not wait for an answer. In a few days I received another letter from him filled with ideas— and later another letter, and so on. It was not long before this man was crossing the continent to accept a position in my organization. This came about during a time when there were thousands of unemployed people right in my neighborhood. You see, he wrote with my interest in mind, not his own.

Do not write to one firm only. Select at least ten of them; the kind of firms you would like to be associated with. Write them letters telling what you believe you have to offer which will prove of value to their businesses. If you do not receive an answer within a few days, do not become discouraged, but write another letter, each time adding some new thoughts showing your interest in them. Such a program is certain to bring you a few invitations to call, and from those calls, if your presentation is logically presented, there is a strong likelihood you will land just the job you're after.

CHAPTER SEVENTEEN

How to Build a Business of Your Own

THE OBJECTIVE OF most men, and a good percentage of women, is to eventually have a business of their own. It's a worthy objective, too, and one easier to attain than most of us realize.

If it is your objective to have your own business, this chapter will put you on your way. If you are not quite ready for such a step, then you might skip this chapter, coming back to it when your attitude regarding a business changes.

Most businesses are built on ideas. In fact every business in existence today is built around a basic idea. And, ideas are something which many of us feel belong to a chosen few. Ask the first ten people you come in contact with if any one of them feels he has an idea on which a business could be built and you will probably not find more than one. And, should you question that one, you are likely to find that he has little or no confidence in his own ideas—otherwise he would have made use of them.

Since ideas form the foundation of most businesses, I will take the first several pages to talk about them—and particularly how to develop sound, workable ideas.

Ideas are the spark plugs of success. Fortunes, industry, even empires have been built on ideas. None of us will belittle the value of good constructive ideas, but the strange thing is, you will find very few people who have faith enough in themselves to give any value to their ideas.

"If that idea was any good, someone else would have thought of it." This expression has been used so many times it is threadbare. Perhaps you have said it in the past, but never again in the future, I am sure.

Let us first consider the value of ideas, then I will show you how to make your mind a veritable fountain of ideas.

A man opened a market in a small country town. The community was so small he could not do more than make a scanty living if he had all the town's business. He got a list of every person living within 35 miles of his store and started a mail campaign directing attention to all the fine things he had for them. He provided ample parking provisions and even a play-yard for children. That man developed a business of over $300,000 per year—more, perhaps, than all of the other merchants in that town put together. He had an idea and he made use of it.

In these United States there are countless thousands of restaurants, many of which are just getting by. There are, however, certain ones which have become known throughout the entire country because they built ideas into their businesses. I take many transcontinental motor trips, and I have my favorite eating places in nearly every section of the country, and I find they must be the favorite places

of many other people because they are always well patron-
ized.

A young man who had been a pressman in a printing
plant decided he would go into business for himself. The
printing business, like restaurants, is a highly competitive
business. This man decided that, instead of organizing a
plant to take care of all kinds of printing, he would spe-
cialize in just one kind of forms. Instead of needing press
equipment of all kinds, and buying paper for many purposes, he could start with but one press and most of his
paper was of one kind. Specializing as he did, he had his
plant set up so that he could undersell most competition.
His business climbed and he was able to retire, a rich man,
when in the early forties.

Every patent in the U.S. Patent Office is the result of
an idea. Where did they come from? From whom did they
come? A large percentage of them emanated from just
plain folk—like you and me. In thinking of patents, it is
often said that there are so many patents it is increasingly
difficult to think up something new. This, of course, is
wrong. Each new patent issued opens up opportunities for
countless new patents. An automobile is made up of thousands of different patents and each day sees new ideas coming into being regarding automotive transportation. With
the invention of radio, an entirely new field of invention
and discovery was opened up. Television has paved the
way for countless hundreds of new inventions. So, as we
think about it, we realize that instead of opportunities for
inventions decreasing, they are multiplying—rapidly.

Every time anything goes wrong, you are facing an opportunity for a new invention. The first can openers were

gadgets which were inserted in the top of a can and pumped up and down, leaving a protruding saw-tooth edge around the top of the can. Many people, in opening a can, would cut a finger and do nothing except, perhaps, say a few naughty words. One man, instead of feeling sorry over a cut finger, asked himself why a can opener could not be made which would leave a smooth edge. He found no negative answer to this question, so he went to work and invented an instrument which not only saved people from cutting themselves, but netted him a neat fortune in addition.

We might refer to ideas as crystallized thought; thought which has taken form; a foundation on which to build. Every place you look you see ideas which have become realities. Every business is built on an idea. Everything you buy came from an idea. The clothes you wear, the house in which you live, the automobile you drive—all resulted from ideas.

You can struggle all of your life without making much progress—when suddenly a single idea can lift you out of obscurity into the limelight of success and happiness.

There is no age limit to those who might develop ideas of value. In fact, many people in the 60's, 70's, and even beyond, have conceived ideas which have enabled them to make more progress in a limited time than they had made throughout all of their previous years.

In my own personal case I might say that my greatest progress in life was after I had passed the 50-year mark. Age is often an advantage instead of otherwise. The knowledge one gains through the years "seasons" the mind so that one may better evaluate his ideas.

I know I am right in assuming that you have within your mental equipment all that is necessary to enable you to develop ideas which will be of definite value to humanity, and which also will reap handsome rewards for you.

Following are five steps designed to help you bring valuable ideas into being. Read them carefully and thoughtfully.

STEP ONE.   Before we can do anything we must *know* we can do it. This is just as true with the formation of ideas as it is to the making of a tangible object. So, we must first begin by *knowing* that we are fully capable of conceiving ideas of definite value. We have already learned that the proper way to create an awareness of any truth is by so instructing the mental self through the use of appropriate affirmations. The development of ideas will be no exception. Become thoroughly relaxed and repeat the following statement and, as you are doing so, sense the truth of every word you are expressing. *"My mind is alert and active, continually bringing into consciousness a flow of constructive ideas of value to humanity."*

It might be well to commit this affirmation to memory and, whenever you are doing anything of a creative nature, repeat it to yourself.

STEP TWO.   The step just concluded will aid you in conditioning your mind so that you will be able to develop constructive ideas. The purpose of this step is to cause you to become *idea conscious*. Develop a curious mind. While I do not recommend that you become disgruntled with everything you see, I do suggest that you form a habit of thinking in terms of improvement. When you have contact with anything, think of it in terms of "What can be done to improve this, or make it better?"

If you are employed, study the work you are doing. How can it be done better? Faster? Approaching your work with such an attitude will make it far more enjoyable, as well as building within yourself the confidence you will need when entering your own business. Your time will pass more quickly and pleasantly, and, from your constructive thinking, ideas may come into being which will reward you handsomely for your greater interest. Do not approach your work in this manner solely from a selfish standpoint. Do so for the stimulation which comes to one when a job is well done. The less you work for a reward, the more certain it is to come to you.

STEP THREE. The purpose of this chapter is to arouse you to the point of *knowing* you are capable of valuable ideas, and to show you how to make the greatest use of them. The suggestion paramount in this step is that you weigh each idea coming into consciousness as to its practicality. In the beginning, some ideas presenting themselves to you may be born of wishful thinking. Your desire for a certain condition may bring into mind thoughts which, on the surface, may appear as happy solutions. Think through on the ideas and if, after careful reflection, they appear sound and practical to you, put them into effect without delay.

Ideas may occur to you which will require effort on your part in putting them into operation. To others they may offer opportunities for procrastination, but not with you. With your determination and self-mastery, that which may appear as labor to another will be welcomed by you because it means growth and achievement.

STEP FOUR. An idea becomes something tangible the moment you do something about it. In the past, many worthwhile ideas have flowed through your mind just as so much water will run under a bridge. An idea has its greatest intensity at the time of its birth. Preserve it before it begins to fade. Start an idea file. Each time an idea comes into your consciousness, unless you are so situated that you can make use of it at once, write it down. Write down everything which comes into mind regarding that idea. The very act of writing it down gives life to the idea and prevents it from fading. If the idea can be pictured, and you are at all adept with a pencil, make a sketch of it. Remember, the more you do regarding the idea, the bigger it grows and the more likely you are to do something about it. It will be well to review the ideas in your file at intervals to keep them alive in your mind. Also, should you gain thoughts which apply to ideas already in your idea file—be sure to record those thoughts, too.

STEP FIVE. A dormant idea is of no value. It is like having a surplus of food which is spoiling while many people are starving.

The average mind is capable of conceiving far more valuable ideas than any one individual can make use of. To hoard ideas merely in hope that some day they may bring revenue to you is not too wise. Under such circumstances you are not gaining any compensation, and humanity at large has failed to benefit through your creative forces. You will agree with this, I am sure.

The more we give in life, the more we get. This is true

regarding ideas. The moment we can establish the fact that we have valuable ideas, we will be called upon from various sources for our ideas. If an idea comes to you which you cannot make use of at the moment, why not give it to the individual or firm who can use it? You will be amazed at the rewards which will come to you as a result of your generosity.

You might think of a way that a certain product can be improved. If you are not in a position to use the idea, why not present it to some manufacturer of that product? After you find your ideas are being used, you will have more confidence in yourself, and as a result, more, and perhaps even better, ideas will flow to you.

Now Let's Think About Your Own Business

The text of this chapter so far seems to be more of a floundering around than any specific plan for gaining a business of your own. It was done intentionally. Since businesses are based upon ideas, and their success depends upon a continual flow of ideas, it is desirable that you gain an *idea consciousness*—that state of mind where you *know* you are a veritable fount of constructive ideas.

In starting to plan a business of your own, there are several questions which must be answered, namely:

1. *What business would you like?* This seems like an elementary question, yet it is an important one. There are so many people who are always bemoaning the fact they can't have a business of their own, yet, when asked the kind of a business they would like, they do not know.

In reaching the objective of owning and operating a

business, one must know exactly the type of a business he wishes to own. He should see it so clearly in his mind that it almost appears as a reality.

2. *Have you the necessary experience?* A prominent financial publication stated that of the many reasons why some businesses fail, the two most common are: (1) insufficient capital, and (2) lack of experience.

Just because you like a business and *feel* you could make good in one is no sound reason that you could. Experience is so vital, it would be better to postpone the start of your business until you become experienced.

There are many ways of gaining experience. First of all, get good books on the subject; subscribe to one or more trade magazines in the field of your interest. And, in addition, seek an opportunity of putting your theories into practice. It is often possible to work, in your spare time, for a firm similar to the one in which you are interested. In addition to the theory you will be acquiring, you will get the *feel* of the business.

3. *Have you sufficient capital to start your business?* Hundreds of men and women have told me that the only reason they are not in business for themselves is because they lack the necessary money to do so. Perhaps many who will read this book up to this point will agree they would like to be in a business of their own—but they haven't the cash required. Perhaps an illustration I might give will prove an inspiration to all such people.

A young man once came to me and actually pitied himself because he had to work for others and not for himself. He explained that with his normal expenses it was impossible for him to put away a cent. Every time he would get a dollar ahead, sickness or something unforeseen would appear and take the money away.

While he was talking I saw a small cardboard box near by. I picked it up and cut a slot in the lid and then with my pen lettered: "Fund for a business of my own." Without showing him what I had done, I asked him for a coin —any coin. He pulled out some small change and handed me a quarter. I dropped it into the slot, handed the box to him and said: "Your new business fund is now started— you're on your way." I extracted a promise from him to the effect that of every sum of money he received in the future, he would take something from it and put in the box.

Saving, you know, is a habit—just as spending is. This lad got the habit. It was not long until the small change had grown to $10. Then his next objective was to make it reach $100, then a thousand, etc. As he saw his savings grow, and a business of his own looming up on the horizon, he began finding ways and means of adding still more money to his fund. He sought extra work he could do in his spare time. He began to economize on many of the expenditures he at first thought were necessary, and which could now be eliminated.

In brief, it was a comparatively short time until this fellow had the necessary money to enable him to establish a business of his own. And, there's a big satisfaction in knowing that everything you have is of your own making. Building a business on inherited or borrowed money does not provide nearly the thrill one will get when he knows his own ingenuity and ambition is responsible for his success.

STARTING A BUSINESS THE PART TIME WAY

It would make good reading to have the story behind many of our great enterprises. It would be found that many of them started in the home.

One of New Jersey's large real estate firms was started in business in a private home by the mother of two small children. Most of her contacts were made over the telephone, and often she would have a child asleep on her lap while she would be talking to a prospect about buying a house.

Hobby shops are frequently responsible for businesses. Often a man will hit on an item which will prove popular among friends, and, so encouraged, will place it in a few stores with the result that later an independent business is born.

In northern California a young couple became interested in weaving. The husband, with a few power tools, built the looms and his wife gave lessons teaching others how to weave. The business expanded to a point where a factory was built to make the looms and the wife conducts a large studio for teaching.

A large furniture factory had its roots in a small woodworking hobby shop. The owner started by making simple garden furniture and displayed the finished pieces on his lawn. His business grew to a point where he rented outside quarters; kept adding new items of manufacture and now operates a full-sized furniture factory.

A well-known perfume was originally made in the back room of a drug store. The assistant, during times when there were no customers to wait on, would experiment with perfumes. He now heads a fast growing business in that field.

THE PRICELESS INGREDIENT

The most important ingredient in any business venture is enthusiastic self-confidence. With it, the sky is really the limit so far as accomplishment is concerned. Without it, one can—and often will—fail, even with the best of ideas, and yes, even financial backing.

Husband and wife combinations are often very effective. Whenever you see a husband and wife with one objective, you often see a couple not only making money, but one which is gaining real happiness in life.

Among my acquaintances is a couple whose business is making toys. In their home they have a fairly well equipped woodworking hobby shop. The husband designs and makes the toys—his wife paints and decorates them.

Another couple has the sales agency for a good product. The wife keeps the books and handles the telephone orders while her husband calls on the trade.

In southern California is a small mail-order publishing house consisting of a man and wife. The man sets the type and does the printing, his wife handles the mail and fills the orders. It is hard to believe, but it was given on good authority that this family organization is netting $20,000 annually.

As given earlier in this chapter, decide on the business you want; arrange to gain the necessary experience; lay out a program which will enable you to acquire the capital you need, and then add the priceless ingredient—*enthusiastic self-confidence.*

Get yourself in the frame of mind where you will make an exciting game of the venture. Naturally, making money is an essential—but it will actually be secondary to the pride you will take in putting over a business of your own. It is a psychological truth that it is easier to make money when we are doing so for the fun of making it, than when we struggle because we feel we have to have it. And such an attitude will keep you from making money your god—a condition which will rob you of the happiness that can come from personal accomplishment.

CHAPTER EIGHTEEN

How to Master Habits

THIS CHAPTER IS not a preachment. It will tell you how to master habits, but it will not suggest that you give up any habit. If you have a habit, and feel that the pleasure you get from it is worth more than the price it exacts from you, keep it. Your habits are your business—not mine. If you have a habit and genuinely wish to overcome it, the information about to be given to you will show you how to overcome habits without any mental or physical pain. Although the chapter will be devoted to the ways and means of overcoming the tobacco and liquor habits, the same line of reasoning can be applied to all habits.

HOW ABOUT SMOKING?

All right—light up a cigarette, make yourself comfortable, and let us talk about smoking. No, I'm not going to tell you to stop smoking. If you smoke—and enjoy it—and prefer not to stop, you stay just as you are and don't permit anyone to interfere with your habit.

I smoked cigarettes for more years than I like to admit. Perhaps I started smoking them before you were born. I reached a point where I smoked about 50 cigarettes a day. That's a lot of cigarettes. If you are one of those who are interested in visual statistics, I'll tell you how much I smoked. One evening I measured the length of a cigarette and estimated how many of them I have smoked in a lifetime. Would you believe it, I have smoked 114,063 feet of cigarettes? And king sized were not popular then, otherwise this measurement would be at least a fifth more. So what? That's no argument for quitting the habit. I have consumed thousands of gallons of water—but I don't intend to stop drinking it.

Shortly after entering the field of radio, a young lady wrote to me asking how she could stop smoking cigarettes. If she had known how my own lungs reeked with the products of combustion, I am sure she would have sought information elsewhere. But I did know *how* to stop smoking —although I had never made use of the information. I sent my formula to this little lady, not mentioning, of course, that I was pulling on a cigarette while dictating my letter to her.

About four months later I received a letter from this radio friend and every line expressed gratitude. She had overcome her cigarette habit and could not thank me enough. I was genuinely thrilled to learn I had helped her, but gave no thought to using the formula on myself.

Some months later I received another letter—also from

a young lady—conveying the same request. Will I please tell her how she can quit cigarettes? Instead of answering her by mail, I gave the formula on one of my broadcasts— so that many people could be helped. Frankly, I felt a bit guilty in telling people how to stop smoking when I, myself, was seeped in tobacco. I did ease my conscience a bit by adding over the air: "I am not preaching and telling you what you should do. If you smoke and enjoy it, that is your business. What I am telling you is intended for those who have the habit and who wish to overcome it."

After a few weeks, letters came trickling in from those who tried my recipe and who were enjoying freedom from the cigarette habit. This made me happy, of course, yet I continued expecting my heart to pump clean blood when I provided my lungs with nothing but smoke-filled air.

Success stories do travel, and it wasn't long before my name had been linked with many who had stopped smoking. More letters came to me asking me to repeat the sure-fire formula.

Once more I told my listening audience how to overcome the habit of smoking, ending, of course, with the statement that "this formula is for those who have the habit and who wish to overcome it, etc."

I believe my announcer was partially responsible for what later happened to me. I heard him saying to the technician: "I get a kick out of Ben. He tells his listeners how to stop smoking, and then lights up a cigarette." It does sound foolish, doesn't it? It almost made a hypocrite of me; yet my conscience was clear, because I was giving the magic formula only to those who wished to stop smoking. I had included myself among those who "had no desire to stop."

To make this message a confessional as well as a "scientific treatise" on ways and means of overcoming the tobacco habit, I might say that I actually admired those who would say: "No, thanks, I do not smoke." In reality, I believe I was afraid to try the formula which had proved so successful with others. I was like the timid bather on the beach who knew how delightful it is in the surf, yet who hesitated getting more than his big toe in the water. I had remembered the many evenings, after I had removed my clothing, ready to retire. I would dress again, get out the car and go several blocks for a pack of cigarettes so that I would be prepared with a smoke in the early hours of the morning before stores were opened.

It was a bit of philosophy I gave in one of my broadcasts which caused me to take my own medicine. In a particular talk I said that human beings were minds with bodies (as I have said elsewhere in this book), not bodies with minds. Realizing the truth of this statement, I decided that I was, with my physical being, like many mothers are with their children. I knew I should be the master of my being, yet I was permitting it to master me.

My regular custom had been to arise in the morning and then light a cigarette before my shower. Perhaps, if something in the morning paper caught my attention, I might smoke two or three cigarettes before breakfast. One morning I was about to get a pack of cigarettes when the thought came to me: "Why don't I try my own formula for overcoming the habit?" There being no logical answer to this question, I did.

As you will learn in just a moment, there are several stages to this recipe of mine. Well, I went from stage to stage without the slightest difficulty. Giving up the habit was so easy, I actually felt a bit embarrassed that I had allowed it to control me for so many years.

The Magic Formula

Now then, if you are still in earnest in wanting to overcome the habit of cigarettes, the following will make it easy for you. If you are approaching this with an "I dare you to help me" attitude, well—light up another cigarette and proceed no further in this chapter.

* * *

The grip a cigarette has upon you is both physical and psychological. In the past, when you have tried to stop smoking (and most smokers have tried it), two forces have been working against you: your mind telling you that you can't stop, and your physical being calling for the drugs to which it has been accustomed. The combination has proved too much for you and you find an alibi to justify your weakness as you light up another one.

Let us first consider the physical side of the smoking habit. Do you remember when you started smoking? It made you quite ill, didn't it? In fact, you became ill the first several times you smoked. But you kept at it. You either thought it was smart to smoke, or else someone had told you that smoking was soothing to the nerves. If you had heeded Nature in the beginning, you would not be reading this chapter right now. Nature rebelled against the elements contained in tobacco smoke and tried to let you know they were harmful to you by making you ill, but you paid no attention, and kept on and on.

Nature is not revengeful. She will do her best to let you know when something is not good for you, but if you insist, instead of making you pay an immediate penalty, Nature will build up what the medical profession refers to as a *tolerance,* and will try to make the most of that which you insist on doing. In other words, a physical condition is created whereby your system actually depends upon the drugs and will cause a craving feeling if they are denied. There is another angle to the physical aspects of the smoking habit; that of motion. The human body is seldom motionless. It is natural to keep some parts of the body busy. Smoking, aside from supplying drugs to the system, actually gives one something to do. Taking a package from the pocket, removing a cigarette and lighting it, constantly lifting it to your lips, flicking ashes, etc., all are motions which occupy a certain amount of time.

All right, where does the psychological aspect of smoking come in? Perhaps at times you have observed bad effects from smoking and you have tried to stop it for a time, but the system calling for the drugs, and your hands itching for something to do, give you the feeling that to overcome the habit will require more strength than you possess. You resign yourself to the thought that you are a fiend to the habit—and you can do nothing about it.

Now then, can you see what you are up against when you try to stop smoking? You have a gnawing feeling in your system—almost akin to hunger—reminding you constantly that the drugs from tobacco are being missed. Your hands are restlessly looking for the usual duties coincident to smoking. Your Creative Mind is whispering to your conscious mind: "You can't do it. You're weak. You're a fiend, etc." It looks like an impossible job, doesn't it? Well, it isn't. In fact, you'll master the habit without the slightest difficulty, either mentally or physically. Here is the how.

*   *

Instead of looking at a cigarette as something indispensable, through reasoning, develop a genuine hatred for it; a sincere feeling that you have permitted such a thing to actually control you. The following thoughts will help you in forming a new mental attitude toward that something which one writer described as "a little roll of enchantment, with fire on one end and a fool on the other."

1. Think of that annoying cough you have, and how husky your voice is getting. It is quite likely cigarettes are to blame.

2. If a bit of physical exertion causes you to puff and pant, look at your cigarettes as being guilty. (The first benefit I noticed after stopping cigarettes was my ability to climb hilly streets without becoming out of breath.) Merely blow one puff of smoke through your handkerchief and see the brown stain it will leave. Realize what is happening to your lungs when you are drawing that smoke

through them all day long. No wonder you feel short of breath most of the time. Your lungs are so coated with the products of combustion, fresh air can hardly get through.

3. Think of your loss of self-respect. Not having been able to control this habit has caused you to lose faith in yourself; feeling that, if you were not big enough to master an insignificant cigarette, you could not master the bigger things in life.

4. If you need anything and can't afford it (new shoes, hat or suit, for example), think how many of them you could buy with the money you are throwing away on smokes.

5. Blow smoke into a bottle and permit it to remain there a few hours, then smell of it. If one puff of smoke will cause such a stench, imagine the condition of your lungs.

6. Think of the mess and destruction caused by smoking. Ashes everywhere; burned holes in carpets, upholstery, clothing; scorched tabletops. Property, forests, and even lives are lost through fires started with a burning cigarette.

7. Think how your progress is being retarded through laziness caused by the smoking habit. You have a desire to do a certain thing and you light up a cigarette while you think about it. You smoke that one—then another one. You get no further than the "smoking and thinking" stage.

* * *

After you get yourself in the proper frame of mind regarding cigarettes, you are ready for the next step.

If you are one of those smokers who must have a ciga-rette—or two or three—before breakfast, go for an entire week without taking any smoke until after breakfast. This will be easy, because as you feel the desire for a smoke, you can allay the craving by knowing that in just a matter of minutes you will have your smoke.

The next week you are not to take a smoke until after lunch. This will also be easy, because during the first week you began to realize that your will-power has not died yet—and anyway, it is only a few hours until after lunch, and who can't wait until then for a smoke?

You have already guessed what comes for the third week. Yes, that week you are not to take a smoke until after dinner. By that time you are proud of your ability to exert self-discipline, and you find the routine for that week as easy as the previous weeks. Incidentally, by this time, your system is getting used to a smaller daily quantity of the drugs for smoking, with the result that less craving is felt.

By the end of the third week you have actually mastered the habit. From that point on, it is merely a "mopping up" process. After you have gone a full week without any smok-ing after the evening meal, you begin skipping days. Skip one full day—then smoke; skip two days—then smoke; skip three days—and so on. In my case, after I had skipped four days I had no further desire to return to the "weed." If *you* do—take a smoke—but you will discover that it will be a short time only before the desire is completely gone.

Until you become accustomed to getting along without your cigarettes, you might find it helpful to have some-thing handy to take when the thought of a smoke enters your mind. Some people like to chew gum, others enjoy the sour tang of lemon drops or the slightly bitter taste of horehound. I found the latter helpful when I was going through the stages which gave me my emancipation from the slavery of the cigarette habit.

Now then, my friend, it's up to you. If you want to discover how good it feels to really be the master of your own physical being, instead of permitting it to master you, you have the secret. After you have taken the step, there is no telling how high you might climb, since you have learned how to conquer instead of being conquered.

How About the Liquor Habit?

The same general principles suggested for tobacco can be used in overcoming the liquor habit.

First form a definite dislike for liquor, even to the extent of feeling angry toward yourself every time you touch it. The following thoughts will help you in developing an antipathy toward "demon rum."

1. Check in the newspaper the number of crimes committed by those under the influence of liquor: murders, automobile accidents, fights, domestic quarrels, often resulting in divorce.

2. Think of the effect liquor has on one's reputation. When under the influence of liquor, one will do things and say things which will cause great embarrassment when they meet him face to face after he is sober.

3. Calculate the amount of money one will spend in the

course of a year for alcoholic beverages. $10 weekly is nothing to spend for liquor. This amounts to over $500 annually or almost enough to make the down payment on a new home. I have a hobby shop containing many thousand dollars' worth of power tools. It won first prize by one of the hobby magazines as being the most complete shop of its kind in the country. As complete as this shop is, and as much money as it costs, I found that the money I saved on tobacco and liquor was more than enough to cover the entire investment. On Monday mornings, instead of having a large head and that "oh-why-did-I-do-it" feeling, I feel alert and happy through having spent a constructive weekend among my hobby equipment.

4. Consider the vast number of people who have had their careers upset through the habit. Yes, many people feel they can "handle" their liquor, and that it will never control them, yet all bad cases of alcoholism had a modest start.

5. Think of your loss of self-respect. Each time you indulge too freely, you think a little less of yourself.

* * *

It is a fact that very few people drink alcoholic beverages merely for the taste. To watch the faces of many when they take a drink, you will understand the taste is not the main objective of drinking. Alcohol is a mental anaesthetic. It deadens the mind and gives us freedom from thoughts which might be haunting us. We drink, therefore, to be able to "let down the bars" and have a temporary freedom from thought of a serious nature.

Usually the ones who wish to get away from their thoughts are those who have failed to make good in their work or who have a guilty conscience over acts of the past or present. There are times when idleness will cause a desire for a mental letdown. To find yourself with nothing at all to do will cause mental unhappiness, and liquor might furnish the means of turning a self-accusing mind to a carefree mind. Then, mental laziness may play a part. One might not be busily engaged, yet be too lazy, mentally, to start any activity which would cause mental effort. Here again, alcohol plays a part in relieving the mind of any serious thinking.

You can't take away anything without replacing it with something, because Nature abhors a vacuum. If you are going to seriously overcome your liquor habit, you'll be far more successful if you replace it with something.

Reginald Denny, the well-known movie and television actor, at one time had a store in Hollywood dealing in materials for the hobbyist—and particularly for those interested in model airplanes.

A friend of Denny's, who was on the verge of being an alcoholic, visited his store. This fellow was one of those who worked all day and the minute he reached home would get out the bottle and drink all evening—going to bed well intoxicated. Throughout the night he'd succeed in sleeping it off to an extent which permitted him to return to business the next day. However, he was fast reaching the point where his efficiency dropped to such an extent he was on the verge of losing his job.

Reginald encouraged his friend to try his hand in building a model airplane. The tiny little parts used in building the plane require a steady hand in assembling them, and the few drinks this fellow had taken on his arrival home made his hand shake to a point where he had difficulty with the miniature pieces. But he was interested. The next evening he began working on his project before taking his first drink, and he continued for several hours without a drink. It was only a short time before the bug had bitten him so badly he had no further desire to drink. You see, he had found something to take the place of liquor which meant more to him than the mental stupor he had been bringing on nightly. And this was not all of his reward. The money he saved since conquering the habit, enabled him to take far better care of his family. A further, and perhaps more valuable result, was the new found happiness which had come into his home.

In mastering the liquor habit, it might be the best idea to proceed in the same manner as suggested for overcoming the cigarette habit. Do it on a step-by-step basis. Go one day without a drink, then two days, three days, four days, and so on. Keep extending the time until the desire is gone.

To have something to look forward to, decide on something you would like to have, but never felt you could afford. Take at least part of the money you have been spending for liquor and lay it aside for your new objective. Your objective mav be a new car; a wardrobe of fine clothes; a television receiver—or even a new home. It will amaze you how fast the liquor money will accumulate.

Conquering the habit will not be your only satisfaction. Naturally your health will improve. And the progress you will make in your job or business will add greatly to your financial standing

CHAPTER NINETEEN

How to Find the Right Mate

A YOUNG LADY once came to me with the question: "How can I find a husband?" She was surprised when I answered her by saying: "The best way to get a husband is to stop looking for one." I followed this answer by telling her that instead of looking for a husband, she should make her own life so complete that she could be happy, even if she didn't have a husband. Then I added that if she would make herself the type of a woman a man would want as a wife, her problem would soon be choosing from those who are seeking her. She understood what I was leading up to and followed my suggestions. It seemed only a short time when she was radiantly happy as she told me she was engaged to be married to "the finest man in town."

This is true with both sexes. We might get a husband or a wife if we intentionally set out looking for one, but marriages based on such "discoveries" seldom last.

It is strange, but true, that the average eligible man or

woman will shy away from the one intentionally set on matrimony. On the other hand, when a man sees a woman who seems to possess everything it takes to make a successful wife, and who seems satisfied to stay as she is, he will, if he runs true to form, make a concerted effort to win her. And, of course, the reverse is true. A woman is always more interested in the man who appears independent so far as marriage is concerned than she is in the man who is ready to propose the second time a girl smiles at him.

THE THREE PHASES OF A HAPPY MARRIAGE

A happy marriage is built around three distinct phases: Mental, Physical and Spiritual, and, like a three-legged stool which will fall if any one of the three legs is removed, so, too, will a marriage fail if it is not based on these three phases.

To be *mentally compatible* does not necessarily mean that two people must think alike. It means that they must be satisfied with the type of thinking each one employs. If a man is of the plodder type, one content to follow the same groove year in and year out, he would soon become unhappy with the woman with a mind too alert and progressive. On the other hand, the go-getter type of a man would find fault with the wife who had a closed mind, one not willing to listen to anything associated with the march of time.

Extraverts and introverts can be happy together. The

extravert might find comfort, after an active day on the outside, to arrive home to the introvert and talk about things akin to the soul. The introvert will gladly break the monotony occasionally by taking a fling out in the world with an extravert husband.

To be *spiritually compatible* does not necessarily mean that a couple should have the same religion. It means they should be on a par so far as their religious interests are concerned. A man with but little religion could become very much bored with a wife who was constantly engaged in some church activity. And of course, such a wife could not be too happy if she had a husband who would take no interest in her chuch work.

Please remember, there are exceptions to every rule. In a work of this kind the thoughts must be confined to generalities. I know a couple—extremely happy—and the husband never sees the inside of a church, whereas his wife spends many, many hours each week participating in various church activities.

The *physical* side of marriage is, and unfortunately so, the phase which is considered more than the other two in most unions. Most cases of infatuation grow out of the stimulation which comes from physical contact. The squeeze of the hand, the kiss, the embrace—all contribute to that emotional state which we refer to as love.

Stimulation from physical contact is necessary—definitely so—but without mental and spiritual compatibility a union will soon head toward the rocks. Many, many husbands and wives will report frigidity on the part of the mate. They will so often relate that when first married, it did not exist—but now no affection at all is forthcoming.

When a marriage is based on the three essentials—Mental, Spiritual and Physical—each phase keeps the other two actively alive. If a union is based on sex alone, like a child with a toy, the newness will wear off and there is nothing left to cling to. But close harmony, mentally and spiritually, will keep the physical phase of marriage glowingly active.

What Should a Woman Look for in a Man?

If humans were as careful in selecting their mates as they are in choosing an automobile, the divorce rate would drop materially. In buying a car, one will not only consider looks, but durability, performance, economy, etc. With a man or woman, if the one of the opposite sex is appealing in one or more ways, a state of infatuation exists and the two feel certain of their love.

Before proceeding it is well to point out that no one will ever find perfection in a mate. Allowances must always be made, but if the attraction is based on sound fundamentals it will be easy, and even enjoyable, to make the allowances.

A young man came to me for counsel regarding a girl he had been keeping company with. He did love her for many things, but he couldn't quite reach the point of proposing because of a few details which did not seem quite right. She was a good girl—he admitted that. She had lots of charm, could cook well, was economical, and a good housekeeper. But—and then he mentioned a few little, actually minor, things, which were not exactly to his liking. It was evident he was seeking perfection.

After he told me his story and was waiting for my answer, I surprised him by asking him a question. "Do you think," I asked, "you could give this girl perfection?" Unhesitatingly he replied, "No." Then I asked him why he thought he should be entitled to find perfection in a girl. He saw my point and married the girl; and as far as I have been able to learn "has lived happily ever after."

When genuine love exists, it is not only easy to overlook little faults, but one can actually reach a state of mind where he loves the little faults because they are part of the one so near and dear to him.

In accepting one as a life partner, a person will be a bit safer if he will permit his head—as well as his heart—to assist toward reaching the all important decision.

In appraising a man, with matrimony as an objective, were I a woman I believe I would give considerable thought to the following characteristics. As I said, I would not expect perfection in all of them, but by taking each attribute in consideration I would at least be using more than average intelligence in entering a life partnership.

1. *The Three Essentials.* More important than anything else is to look for compatibility regarding the mental, spiritual and physical phases. To make any compromise in this direction is courting with danger.

2. *Integrity.* Every woman likes to feel that her hus-

band is reliable, trustworthy and possesses the type of character which demands respect from others. A man who will guard his honor among those in the outside world is more than likely to be honorable in his home.

3. *Industrious.* A wife seldom has reason to feel insecure if married to an industrious man. Some men are industrious to the extent they even spend many of their spare time hours in furthering their work. While such a man may deprive his wife of his company during the early years of marriage, he is often the type which can provide comforts and luxuries in later years of marriage. The pendulum, however, can swing just as far in one direction as it can in the other. One can make a mistake by working too hard, just as he can by leaning too heavily on the "loafing" side.

4. *Ambitious.* There is a difference between ambition and industry. One can be very industrious and yet not too ambitious. He might be content to follow in the same groove for years without attempt for self-improvement. I believe a woman would be wise to think about a man's ambition. It is a satisfaction to a woman to see her husband constantly improving his station in life.

5. *Good provider.* A man might be industrious and ambitous and yet not be a good provider. There are men who allow so little money for household expenses, it is impossible for the wife to properly set her table, or dress herself and family. It is not difficult for the average woman to earn enough to take proper care of herself. Therefore

she would not be happy to be faced with a permanent situation whereby she is not provided with as good as she would be able to obtain if single. Many women have independent incomes through their own occupations. This should not in any way relieve the husband of the responsibility of providing the basic food, shelter and raiment.

6. *Generous.* A husband, to give a woman the sense of security she deserves, should be thrifty. It is possible, however, for a man to be generous and yet thrifty. If he handles his income on a proper budget basis, he can usually be generous and yet lay aside a bit for future objectives. Generosity does not necessarily apply wholly to finances. One can be generous with his love and affection, friendship, cooperation, etc.

7. *Understanding.* Perhaps this is the most important word in the lexicon of the lover. We might define the word as meaning: knowing why we are as we are. There will seldom be misunderstanding where there exists understanding. Sounds like a paradox, doesn't it? Being a bit specific, it might be pointed out that most quarrels result from a lack of understanding. We judge by acts, not the motives in back of the acts.

Every act is justified in the mind of the one committing the act at the time the act was performed. This applies to everything—even murder. I am not implying that the acts were right, but the one responsible for the act felt justified in doing it at the time. Burglars often steal because they feel Fate has discriminated against them and they take it upon themselves to collect from the world that to which they feel entitled. Their acts, of course, are wrong —but not in their minds.

A husband may arrive home at night feeling rather irritable. His wife may take it as an affront and "put him on the spot" for his disposition. The understanding wife, before allowing herself to become quarrelsome as a result of the husband's attitude will reason that he might have had some problems during the day which exhausted his patience. This kind of a wife will tactfully refrain from referring to the touchy subject and, instead, will do everything she can to make her husband comfortable and enable him to forget the trials of the day.

Yes, in appraising your prospective mate, do a little checking regarding his understanding—or lack of it.

8. *Disposition.*   A woman was discussing her fiance with me. She told me about a few of his idiosyncrasies; in fact, she said, she could not even mention them to him because he would fly off the handle when she would do so. Even knowing the kind of a disposition her friend had, she was still contemplating marrying him. Many women make the mistake of feeling a man will change after marriage. Yes, he does change, but not always for the better. If he can get away with a bad disposition before marriage, it is quite likely to grow worse after marriage.

A bad disposition is one of the worst handicaps a person can have. It is highly possible to be happy with a person who is physically handicapped, but not with one with a bad disposition.

Of course, dispositions can change. A bad disposition is

not a cause, it is an effect; and sometimes if we know what has been causing it, a correction might be made which would overcome it. But do not be an optimist to the extent of feeling it will change by itself. If you can find the cause of the bad disposition and help your friend to change—fine. But, for the sake of your future happiness, unless the disposition has definitely changed—watch out.

9. *Habits.* Some women enjoy going to night clubs and bars with their boy friends before marriage, and even think it "cute" to see him get tight. It may be well to realize that this may be a forerunner to a life of drinking after marriage. It is pathetic to know the thousands and thousands of couples living in poverty because liquor is taking the bulk of their income. So, in considering marital possibilities, make certain that there will be no habits robbing you of your deserved happiness.

10. *Clean—mentally and physically.* It is not too easy to determine this characteristic before marriage, because one will guard against giving a wrong impression in this direction. However, through keen observation it is possible to determine the tendencies regarding cleanliness. In time, little tell-tale indications will reveal whether the apparent cleanliness is natural, or just a front.

11. *Parental attitude.* Does he like children? Will he make a good father? These are questions which should be answered, because it is natural for normal women to look forward to motherhood.

A childless mother bemoaned the fact that her husband

would not permit her to have a baby. She said she had always looked forward to having a home and children. I asked her what his attitude regarding children had been before marriage. She admitted she had not discussed that with him before they married.

If you are looking forward to a home with children, it would be prudent to make sure that the man of your choice has the same desire.

12. *Health?* No one can blame a person who becomes ill. Many wives or husbands who have the correct feeling toward each other will actually be drawn closer together through illness. This, of course, applies to illness contracted after marriage. Some people are frequently ill because of the neglect of their health and the manner in which they live. If your boy friend is one of those constantly ailing, it would be wise to be a bit cautious. There are, you know, such things as psychosomatic ills which come as a defense. Not having sufficient ambition to accomplish big things, an illness will provide a fitting out.

13. *Is he fair?* A man might have all the qualities so far discussed and yet cause heartaches through not being fair to his mate. For example, a man of my acquaintance has the finest array of expensive guns and fishing tackle of any man I know. Nearly every week end will see him going on some hunting or fishing trip—alone, of course. He has never bought his wife a sewing machine, a vacuum cleaner, a washing machine, or other household utilities. He thinks he is fair because he provides her with a roof over her head and sufficient food, but he never realizes

that all income should be considered as community income and that she should enjoy a few of the luxuries just as he does.

There are other places to exhibit fairness, too. A man should do his part in looking after the house and children. Of course you can't determine such things in advance of marriage except by speculation. However, observation will give a fair idea of one's fairness or lack of it.

*   *   *

The foregoing thoughts do not cover all desirable characteristics by any means. But, they will cause your mind to run in the channels which will give you a picture, quite clear, of the man you may consider as a husband.

WHAT SHOULD A MAN LOOK FOR IN A WOMAN?

Being a man, it is a bit simpler to outline those traits which a woman should possess in order to enhance the possibility of a happy marriage. Here are some of the things I believe a man should look for.

1. *The Three Essentials.* Just as suggested for the woman, so too, should a man make certain there will be complete compatibility so far as the mental, spiritual and physical aspects of marriage are concerned. This is of basic importance.

2. *Understanding.* This item comes earlier in the list of traits to look for in a woman than it did in the other

list. And, it is right that it should take honor place. I believe understanding is one of the most valuable traits a woman can have. A man once told me he had not had a quarrel with his wife in the ten years they were married. Then he added that if they had quarreled it would undoubtedly be his fault because she was the most understanding woman he had ever met. This is a beautiful tribute to be paid to this deserving wife. Everything said regarding understanding in the previous list (Item No. 7) will apply to this checking list.

3. *Managing a home.*   This is an important assignment which falls to the wife in all marriages. Even if wealth is acquired, there will always be the necessity for sound home management. This training can be acquired, so if the girl has not gained the necessary knowledge for home management, she should show her willingness to take steps to learn.

4. *Cooking.*   I think every woman should know how to cook—and well. Some couples start out living in boarding homes where cooking is unnecessary, but, if the husband succeeds in life, he will be acquiring a home of his own where there will be cooking. And even should the budget permit of an employed cook, it is still desirable that the wife should know how to cook. A friend of mine told me that he always looks forward to Wednesday's dinners. That is the cook's day off and his wife does the cooking, and he so thoroughly enjoys her cooking.

5. *Sewing.*   In this day and age it might not seem neces-

sary for a woman to know how to sew. There are many times, however, when the ability to sew will prove invaluable. Women in governmental service have learned the value of knowing how to sew. There are many occasions when it would be impossible for them to locate the services of a seamstress, and unless they could care for their clothes themselves, it would be unfortunate. On vacations, many times an emergency will arise which will prove the value of skill with the thread and needle. Then, many times, women will take delight in remodeling their own clothes, even though their circumstances might permit the services of a seamstress.

6. *Living within one's means.* A man of considerable means once told me that his wife was responsible for their fortune. He said that she was always able to run the house and not only live within their means, but save money as well. On the other hand, a young business man told me that at home he does not dare tell his wife about the things which happen in his office. If he has a poor month and he tells her, she tells him what a poor business man he is. If he has a good month, she runs out to the stores and runs in debt for far more than he earned.

Handling the finances of a family is not a one-sided arrangement at all. Some husbands do not give their wives enough with which to show their saving talent. Others are held back because the wives are too reckless with the money.

7. *Jealousy.* Do not be flattered if the girl of your dreams is jealous of you. Jealousy can rob the happiness

of a marriage more than any other thing. There will be more on this subject in the next chapter.

8. *Sympathetic with husband's work and problems.* Behind nearly every great man is the sympathetic, understanding wife. The woman who shows no interest in your work is likely to prove a handicap in marriage. She will fail to understand the extra hours you will often find necessary to apply to your work. And, it deprives the husband of the pleasure of discussing his business problems with her. I often visit a home where the husband is eager to talk about his work to me because his wife refuses to listen. And this man is frequently finding excuses to go away from home to be with others who will speak his business language.

9. *Good Mother.* Finding a woman who is not looking forward to motherhood is not easy, although there are women who prefer to go through life childless. Should you happen to be a man fond of children, you had better make certain on this point.

10. *Clean and tidy.* Cleanliness is much more common among women than among men. But, should the girl of your choice show tendencies to be other than neat and clean before marriage, you had better give a little thought before dropping to your knees.

11. *Good habits.* Although a woman should have as much right as a man to indulge in bad habits, for some reason we expect women to be better than men. Men will tolerate habits of men which they would abhor in a woman.

Do not accept a state of infatuation whereby you will look at bad habits as "cute." They will become very disgusting after marriage.

* * *

Returning to a thought expressed in the early part of this chapter. Do not intentionally go after a husband or wife. If you are a woman, make of yourself the type of a person the right man would want for a wife. If you are a man, make of yourself the kind of a person the right woman would want for a husband. Your problems will not be seeking a mate—but choosing from those who will be seeking you.

CHAPTER TWENTY

Your Marriage Can Be Happy

Making a Success of Your Marriage Is Proving
Your Leadership in Directing One of the Greatest
Institutions on the Face of the Earth.

IT IS NEVER necessary to stop anything one doesn't start.
If a couple, about to be married, will pledge to each other
they will follow a prescribed pattern throughout their
married lives—a pattern designed to promote happiness—
and avoid friction—there will be no marital heartaches—
and the two will grow closer together as the years pass by.

The first part of this chapter will be dedicated to those
about to enter matrimony. This will be followed by suggestions to those already married, then the chapter will

end with the 10 Commandments for a Happy Marriage
which applies to all married people.

*   *   *

When a man and woman reach that stage of courtship
where to mention the name of the other brings a quicken-
ing of the pulse and a flush of warmth to the cheeks; when
the moments of separation are interminable; when nights
bring dreams of love and devotion—this, indeed, is one's
nearest approach to heaven on earth.

During this blessed period, intentions are good on the
part of both. In their ecstasy there is nothing they would
not do for the other; and the life to follow the wedding
will represent nothing short of a sojourn with the angels

A glimpse of the vital statistics will show that with an
alarmingly large percentage of marriages, the pre-marital
flight into the skies was a snare and a delusion. At least
one-fourth of all marriages end in either divorce or separation, and it is safe to assume that the greater part of those
remaining married are considering ways and means of
changing their marital status. After the wedding knot is
tied, the girl finds that the man she married—the Prince
Charming—is just an ordinary human with feet of clay. He
finds that the girl he married lacks many of the angelic
characteristics his imagination had attached to her. What
a pity! Is marriage a trap, set and ready to spring, crushing
the hearts of the unsuspecting who enter? It need not be so.
It is not so. There is nothing wrong with the institution of
marriage, the fault lies with the attitude of those who enter.

When marriage is consummated, first, with the right

love for each other; secondly, with the correct understanding of the obligations and responsibilities of marriage, and lastly, with the fixed determination to make a success of it, marriage will be found that, instead of ending the emotional thrill of the days of courtship, it will be the opening of the door to a life of increasing and deepening happiness.

There is nothing mystical or magical about the message being given in this chapter, but it does contain a formula—easy to follow—which will insure a continuation of courtship happiness right through until "unto death do you part."

You—about to enter the holy bonds of matrimony—read this chapter carefully—thoughtfully; talk about it to each other; sign the pledge, then start on your blessed road to happiness.

A Word to the Bride

The mere mention of this name brings mental pictures of the white gown with flowing veil coupled to the melodic strains of the wedding march. The marriage in contemplation—and the marriage being performed—right through to the words which seem to come from heaven: "I now pronounce you husband and wife," represent a happiness, newly found. We often speak of friendships which culminated in marriage and this too often proves to be true, especially if we think of the word "culmination" and what it means. Webster says that culmination means "reaching the highest point." To reach the peak of anything leaves us with just one direction to go—down. Marriage, properly entered into, should not be the summit, but the start, of the trail leading upward—on to greater vistas of joy and understanding. Each passing year of marriage should see the man and wife closer together and their love binding them to each other as solidly as the trunk of a tree holds the branches together. As children arrive, they should prove a blessing to the union instead of added hardships and responsibilities.

During the courtship, your fiance calls you by many names of endearment and, undoubtedly, those names are based on what he sees in you and, I might add, he sees you through his mental eyes much more than through his physical eyes. Right at this point it might be well to mention a fact little thought of and, perhaps, little understood. The real *you*—as you have already learned from this book—is not physical, it can't be seen with the human eyes. And, as I said before, when you refer to yourself as "I" or "me," you are not at all referring to your physical body; your arms, legs, body, head, etc., you are referring to your mental or spiritual self.

You might be attractive physically, and before getting to know the real you, your friend, through his imagination, will endow you with all the qualities he hopes to find in you. This means that in the early days of courtship, that which he loves—or thinks he loves, is partly of his own making. If, as he learns to know you better, you project the qualities he gave you, fine; the acquaintanceship grows into friendship and then most likely develops into love.

If you fail to do so, he may become disillusioned and the courtship ends before the peal of the wedding bells is heard. In some cases the groom does not have sufficient time to become acquainted with the *spiritual you* before marriage and reaches the stage of disillusionment after the ceremony, then it's just too bad; either a divorce is sought, or a married life devoid of love is tolerated.

These last thoughts might prove a bit frightening. You might wonder if your friend could become disillusioned as he learns to know you better; but this need not happen, especially if you determine to prevent it from happening.

A girl of my acquaintance bemoaned the fact she could not land a husband. She wanted to get married—desperately—but was making no progress at all. From a physical standpoint she was attractive. She wore good clothes. She had a good education and considerable culture. But her real self was repellent. She was envious, jealous, selfish, conceited, and had a bad disposition on top of it all. "Would you marry someone like you, if you were a man?" I asked. She thought a moment—then blushed and admitted she would not. Then I suggested to her, just as I did to another in the previous chapter, that instead of looking for a husband, she spend her time in making of herself the kind of a wife a good man would want. She did, and it was only a short time before her Prince Charming arrived and asked for her hand in marriage.

Some girls—and this might mean you—wonder just what their boy friend thinks of them. I'm going to tell you something which will surprise you. Instead of trying to figure out what another might think of you, ask yourself the question: "What do I think of myself?" Do not let egotism answer this question—or the answer might be colored by desire rather than fact. Look down deep—consider all of your attributes, your disposition, your tolerance, your understanding. If what you find gives you reason to *like yourself,* you need not worry about others, they will like you, too.

There are two things I would like to discuss which will prove well worthy of your consideration. The first thing is *tolerance.* Picking, nagging, and fault finding are often prompted by intolerance, and you know how much those conditions detract from an otherwise happy marriage. When we are deeply in love, it is natural that we see nothing but perfection; in fact, during the days when our emotions have us in the clouds, one's faults even become virtues; but after marriage, when we take off our rose colored glasses and size up our mates for what we actually find them to be, it is within the realm of possibility that we will then appraise their faults as faults—and endeavor to bring them to the attention of those possessing them. Know that, just as you are not perfect, neither will your husband be perfect. Far better than to be intolerant regarding another's faults is to concentrate on the elimination of your own. Often, through example, your spouse will be inspired to do as you are doing.

Understanding is a big word so far as the number of letters are concerned, but the real bigness lies in its depth of meaning. To be understanding means that you understand why people are as they are, and many times, instead of being critical, you'll actually be sympathetic.

"What thou see-est, so thou be-est," is an age old proverb with a wealth of meaning. When we see faults in people and things, it is generally a reflection of that which we have within. Should we find ourselves about to become critical, it might pay us to pause for a moment to ascertain whether or not we are ever guilty of the same thing. It is surprising how often we will hold our criticism as we recall our own shortcomings. For proof, try it!

And now, dear girl, let's talk about disposition. Would you like a person who had a disposition exactly like yours? If your answer is "yes" you have very little to worry about. If, upon reflection, you find that when conditions are not exactly to your liking, you are ready to make your disposition known, then, I fear, you have a bit of changing to do if you wish to make your marriage a really happy one. Bad dispositions are real enemies in so many ways. They are detrimental to health; it has been definitely established that anger produces poisons in the body. Bad dispositions do more harm to physical beauty than cosmetics can ever cover up. You develop a cold, hard expression about the eyes and mouth. Your voice takes on a cold feeling. Your face moulds into a "sour-puss" expression. And a bad disposition is one of the surest ways of dampening the love and admiration of the one who should mean most to you.

Perfection is a desirable state to look for, but do not attempt to reach it for your mate only. To be a perfectionist to the extent of constantly picking flaws in one's manner of speech, eating, working, etc., is flirting with marital danger. In seeking improvement, think in terms of *us*—not you. To have a mutual desire for self-improvement is a harmonious condition. To concentrate on improving your husband is a sure way of inserting the wedge which will ultimately force you apart, if not to a divorce court, at least to the point of destroying the nearness which might have existed between you. I am certain you agree with me.

It will not be necessary to dwell on the advisability of retaining your neatness. You are well aware of the fact that by being sweet, dainty and effeminate, you win the admiration and love of the one who will mean so much to you. To change after marriage tends toward bringing about that feeling of disillusionment talked about earlier in this chapter.

The latter part of this chapter contains the 10 Commandments for a Happy Marriage. Thousands of couples are finding real happiness through these sound suggestions. Some couples, on the verge of estrangement, have recaptured their original nuptial bliss by applying the thoughts as given. But how much better it is for a couple to begin their marriage according to the commandments? We never have to stop that which we do not start. If you incorporate these rules into your marriage vows, you will gain more genuine happiness from marriage than you may anticipate; even considering your present enthusiasm.

May I point out one weakness of human nature? Most of us, in hearing good advice, will think of someone who should have heard it. We seldom pause to ask ourselves if it does not specifically apply to us. This can happen so far as the 10 Commandments are concerned. Many people, in reading them, will immediately mention the name of someone to whom they apply. In this case, think of yourself only. Imagine this chapter to be one specifically written for you and that the Commandments were written solely to assure you a marriage of bliss. So, read the 10 Commandments carefully; then go over them one by one with the young man of your choice and agree to abide by them. Your marriage will be for life and it will grow more beautiful as the happy years roll by.

Now Let's Talk to the Groom

Since the groom is the logical head of the institution of marriage, it may be felt that he should have been considered ahead of the bride. The custom, however, is to think in terms of Bride and Groom; and, inasmuch as the creed of a gentleman is *ladies first*, we will happily let these paragraphs remain as they are. The grooms will agree, I am sure.

Every organization, every city, state and country, needs a directing hand. Without such, there would be chaos. A marriage, which is in effect an institution, a partnership, needs a directing head, and the husband is the natural one to assume that important role.

It might be well to consider the attributes, obligations and responsibilities of the head of the institution of marriage. A good director is one who faithfully and loyally serves those whom he may be directing to such an extent he merits their cooperation, respect, and even love. This applies to marriage as much as it does to the firm manufacturing automobiles or washing machines. The directing head, who forces his will through tyranny, never has harmony or happiness and as a result seldom remains in power for any worthwhile length of time.

Most people look forward to the day when they may hold a position of power and importance. Stepping into the role of a husband is one of the most important assignments on earth, and, the man who makes a success of his marriage is proving his leadership in directing the greatest institution on the face of the earth. The happiness of the loved one, taken in a vow given before God and man, is dependent upon the husband. And the influence the family might exert in the neighborhood, whether for good or bad, is largely dependent upon the husband. To be a good husband one must have unusual powers and a high degree of self-mastery. If conditions are not quite as happy as they might be in the household, instead of quickly blaming his mate for the underlying faults, he must be big enough to realize that in some respect his leadership is faulty and will look for the remedy within himself instead of trying to shift responsibility. He will know that his real great strength is reflected in his gentleness and tenderness toward those whose lives are in his keeping.

In my study of men I have found that those who wield the most power in the business world are frequently the kindliest in their homes. The man who is down-trodden in the business world—the ne'er-do-well—is more often the blustery, bully type in the home. This man, not having the strength of character to stand up for his rights with men, to satisfy his ego that there is someone he can dominate, will do the cowardly thing of acting the tyrant toward his wife and family.

The philanthropist, Andrew Carnegie, once said he would not waste his time in helping lame dogs over fences, which is another way of saying that it is a waste of time helping those who will not try to help themselves. The very fact that you have read this far is an indication of your sincerity in wanting to make your marriage an outstanding success, and it is people like you I like to help.

In the paragraphs addressed to the Bride which you might or might not have read, I touched on the subject of a bad disposition and I am certain the Bride will find it wise to abide by the suggestions given. There are a few thoughts on this subject—and from an entirely different angle, which I should like to pass on to you.

Men, if at all inclined toward flare-ups, have a number of reasons to lose their mental equilibrium, unless they exert the self-control which contributes so much toward their leadership. And the early morning is when the tops blow off. Many psychologists amusingly brand these daybreak tantrums as the *early morning grouch*. But, from a psychological standpoint, our anger, in reality, is not directed toward the harmless piece of toast which, perhaps, is a bit too brown; nor the coffee which might have cooled a degree or two. The anger which upsets the serenity of the home, causing tears in the eyes of your loved one and marring your own day, is caused by a condition from within, not on account of the trifling things toward which you direct it. If you understand the internal forces which cause the upheaval, you will be able to correct the cause, thereby eliminating the effect. I will mention a few reasons which can cause an *early morning grouch,* because I know you will want to avoid them, not only to enable you to make a greater success of your marriage—but to actually help you to make a greater success of your life.

There are three principle factors contributing to an *E.M.G.* I will take them in the order in which they usually appear.

First. Unfinished tasks are never pleasant to anticipate. Many people are good starters but poor finishers. They are always starting things, but as soon as the task becomes a bit hard, they tackle something else. Continually facing a myriad of unfinished jobs is mentally disturbing—and particularly early in the morning. When we awaken and realize that with the new day we must see all of these partly finished jobs pointing accusing fingers at us, well, isn't that reason to be grouchy? The pity of it is that we may not realize what is making us irritable, so we unconsciously look for something on which we might let off the steam we have been accumulating. This is why the toast, coffee or eggs get the fireworks which are psychologically intended for our own weakness in not finishing that which we might have, with good intentions, started. It will pay you well to cultivate the habit of following through on the things you start. Your rewards will be great. You will accomplish much more, and you will eliminate one of the causes of marital inharmony.

Second. Worries are not conducive to a peaceful mind. When one allows himself to worry, his worry does not cease when he drops off to sleep. His subconscious—Creative Mind—carries on where his conscious mind leaves off. In the morning he awakens feeling only half-fit, and is usually ready to find fault on the slightest provocation. However, just as is the case with unfinished tasks, the direction of the anger means little. And, unfortunately, under such circumstances, the husband often says cutting things to his loved one which, down in his heart, is not meant at all, but which in reality should be directed toward himself. Since worry cannot possibly help any condition, the man built of the stuff of which leaders are made—instead of worrying, will take that time in finding a solution to the problem causing the worry.

Third. A guilty conscience is probably responsible for more bad dispositions than any other thing, but that need not be of too much concern to you. We never have to stop anything we do not start, so, in just starting your life as a husband, your sane judgment will prevent you from doing anything which will trouble your conscience. You will never do anything away from home which you would not be happy to do in the presence of your beloved.

It has been said, and correctly so, that, if we can keep happy—and smiling—until 10 o'clock in the morning, the rest of the day will take care of itself. Make this your rule, Mr. Groom, and do not let anything interfere to upset your schedule. Marriage with you is not merely a matter of convenience. You are entering matrimony to prove to yourself and the world at large that you are a leader. One of the greatest compliments which can be paid to any man is to call him a good husband and a good father. That he is a good husband and a good father is proof positive that he is a good man; one to be relied upon, and one who will make his mark in the world.

In discussing the groom, I have dwelt largely on good humor, because it is one of the finest traits a husband can have. A kindly, gentle, understanding husband can bring more happiness to a wife and children than a *meanie*— even though he may possess great wealth.

There is one final thought which may well be added to the Groom's Section: The bride-to-be, in accepting the proposal of marriage, undoubtedly did so with great pride. She accepted you because you represent to her all that any woman could expect to find in a husband. First of all she loves you; her actions prove this. But her love has been moulded around a number of highly desirable attributes. With your ambition and determination to make a success of life, she knows she will grow increasingly proud of you and your accomplishments. To let her down would be letting yourself down, because you *will prove* your leadership in directing the great institution of marriage in every possible way.

Read the 10 Commandments very carefully and then show your bride—or bride-to-be—your earnestness in living according to them; right to the letter.

To Those Already Married

I know of no better suggestion to those already married than to suggest they read very carefully all of the thoughts offered to the bride and groom.

You will at once agree that any couple living according

to such rules will have a happy marriage. You will also
be able to quickly recognize the mistakes you have made
and will know how to correct them.

So, husbands and wives, without further ado, read the
10 Commandments to follow—carefully—and then for just
60 days live according to every one. Your happiness will
be so great you would not wish to return to your former
pattern of life for anything. And, just as I suggested to
and urged the bride and groom to do, sign the pledge; it
will help you materially in keeping your resolution if you,
too, will sign it.

THE 10 COMMANDMENTS FOR A HAPPY MARRIAGE

1. *Keep Yourself Sold to Each Other.*   You created a
good impression before marriage. Continue to create a
good impression after marriage. This is easy to do and the
rewards are great.

2. *It Is More Blessed to Give than to Receive.* In giving, do not be guided by what you might receive in return.
The act of giving should be its own reward. Happiness
comes from giving happiness.

3. *Marriage Should Not Destroy Individuality.*   Entering marriage is a partnership, not ownership of one individual by another. A yoke around the neck soon begins to
chafe.

4. *Never Pry into the Affairs of Your Mate.*   Pockets,
handbags, letters and dresser drawers should be private to
their owners. Suspicion creates inharmony which can have
an unhappy ending.

5. *Never Retire at Night with Any Differences Existing Between You.* A good-night kiss should be a must in every home. This prevents little differences from growing into big ones.

6. *Compliment Each Day.* Giving sincere compliments each day trains you to look for the good things in your mate instead of otherwise. The importance of this commandment cannot be overestimated.

7. *Never Permit Jealousy to Enter Your Home.* When jealousy steps in . . . love walks out. Jealousy and love will not remain together. The more you trust your mate, the more the trust will be deserved.

8. *When Separated Through Circumstances, Write Real Love Letters.* After a couple has been married a few years, an occasional love letter will keep the spark of romance brightly burning.

9. *Operate on a Budget Basis.* Money troubles will often disturb the harmony of a home. Handle your finances sanely. Earn a little, spend a little, save a little. You can be generous with each other . . . yet thrifty.

10. *Be Good to Your In-Laws.* There are two sets of them. If you show love and respect for your in-laws, your mate is most likely to be as considerate of yours. In-laws are real people.

Our Pledge to Each Other

We hereby pledge to ourselves, and to each other, that from this day onward, we will, to the best of our ability, live up to the letter and spirit of the 10 Commandments for a Happy Marriage. Should we at any time, separately or jointly, violate one or more of the commandments, instead of abandoning them, will try much harder to be faithful to them in the future. If either one of us has made any mistakes in the past, those mistakes are wholeheartedly forgiven and will not be repeated or referred to in the future. Our love for each other is genuine and our desire to make an outstanding success of our marriage is sincere. And, since happiness comes from giving happiness, we will do all within our power to influence other couples to follow our example by accepting and living according to these 10 Commandments for a Happy Marriage.

Bride (or Wife) ....

Groom (or Husband) ....

Date ....

MELVIN POWERS SELF-IMPROVEMENT LIBRARY

ASTROLOGY

BRIDGE

BUSINESS, STUDY & REFERENCE

CALLIGRAPHY

CHESS & CHECKERS

___ HOW TO WIN AT CHECKERS *Fred Reinfeld*	5.00
___ 1001 BRILLIANT WAYS TO CHECKMATE *Fred Reinfeld*	7.00
___ 1001 WINNING CHESS SACRIFICES & COMBINATIONS *Fred Reinfeld*	7.00

COOKERY & HERBS

___ CULPEPER'S HERBAL REMEDIES *Dr. Nicholas Culpeper*	5.00
___ FAST GOURMET COOKBOOK *Poppy Cannon*	2.50
___ HEALING POWER OF HERBS *May Bethel*	5.00
___ HEALING POWER OF NATURAL FOODS *May Bethel*	5.00
___ HERBS FOR HEALTH—HOW TO GROW & USE THEM *Louise Evans Doole*	5.00
___ HOME GARDEN COOKBOOK—DELICIOUS NATURAL FOOD RECIPES *Ken Kraft*	3.00
___ MEATLESS MEAL GUIDE *Tomi Ryan & James H. Ryan, M.D.*	4.00
___ VEGETABLE GARDENING FOR BEGINNERS *Hugh Wiberg*	2.00
___ VEGETABLES FOR TODAY'S GARDENS *R. Milton Carleton*	2.00
___ VEGETARIAN COOKERY *Janet Walker*	7.00
___ VEGETARIAN COOKING MADE EASY & DELECTABLE *Veronica Vezza*	3.00
___ VEGETARIAN DELIGHTS—A HAPPY COOKBOOK FOR HEALTH *K. R. Mehta*	2.00
___ VEGETARIAN GOURMET COOKBOOK *Joyce McKinnel*	3.00

GAMBLING & POKER

___ HOW TO WIN AT DICE GAMES *Skip Frey*	3.00
___ HOW TO WIN AT POKER *Terence Reese & Anthony T. Watkins*	7.00
___ WINNING AT CRAPS *Dr. Lloyd T. Commins*	5.00
___ WINNING AT GIN *Chester Wander & Cy Rice*	3.00
___ WINNING AT POKER—AN EXPERT'S GUIDE *John Archer*	5.00
___ WINNING AT 21—AN EXPERT'S GUIDE *John Archer*	7.00
___ WINNING POKER SYSTEMS *Norman Zadeh*	3.00

HEALTH

___ BEE POLLEN *Lynda Lyngheim & Jack Scagnetti*	3.00
___ COPING WITH ALZHEIMER'S *Rose Oliver, Ph.D. & Francis Bock, Ph.D.*	10.00
___ DR. LINDNER'S POINT SYSTEM FOOD PROGRAM *Peter G. Lindner, M.D.*	2.00
___ HELP YOURSELF TO BETTER SIGHT *Margaret Darst Corbett*	7.00
___ HOW YOU CAN STOP SMOKING PERMANENTLY *Ernest Caldwell*	5.00
___ MIND OVER PLATTER *Peter G. Lindner, M.D.*	5.00
___ NATURE'S WAY TO NUTRITION & VIBRANT HEALTH *Robert J. Scrutton*	3.00
___ NEW CARBOHYDRATE DIET COUNTER *Patti Lopez-Pereira*	2.00
___ REFLEXOLOGY *Dr. Maybelle Segal*	5.00
___ REFLEXOLOGY FOR GOOD HEALTH *Anna Kaye & Don C. Matchan*	7.00
___ 30 DAYS TO BEAUTIFUL LEGS *Dr. Marc Selner*	3.00
___ YOU CAN LEARN TO RELAX *Dr. Samuel Gutwirth*	3.00

HOBBIES

___ BEACHCOMBING FOR BEGINNERS *Norman Hickin*	2.00
___ BLACKSTONE'S MODERN CARD TRICKS *Harry Blackstone*	5.00
___ BLACKSTONE'S SECRETS OF MAGIC *Harry Blackstone*	5.00
___ COIN COLLECTING FOR BEGINNERS *Burton Hobson & Fred Reinfeld*	7.00
___ ENTERTAINING WITH ESP *Tony 'Doc' Shiels*	2.00
___ 400 FASCINATING MAGIC TRICKS YOU CAN DO *Howard Thurston*	7.00
___ HOW I TURN JUNK INTO FUN AND PROFIT *Sari*	3.00
___ HOW TO WRITE A HIT SONG & SELL IT *Tommy Boyce*	7.00
___ JUGGLING MADE EASY *Rudolf Dittrich*	3.00
___ MAGIC FOR ALL AGES *Walter Gibson*	4.00
___ MAGIC MADE EASY *Byron Wels*	2.00
___ STAMP COLLECTING FOR BEGINNERS *Burton Hobson*	3.00

HORSE PLAYER'S WINNING GUIDES

___ BETTING HORSES TO WIN *Les Conklin*	7.00
___ ELIMINATE THE LOSERS *Bob McKnight*	5.00
___ HOW TO PICK WINNING HORSES *Bob McKnight*	5.00

___ HOW TO WIN AT THE RACES *Sam (The Genius) Lewin*	5.00
___ HOW YOU CAN BEAT THE RACES *Jack Kavanagh*	5.00
___ MAKING MONEY AT THE RACES *David Barr*	5.00
___ PAYDAY AT THE RACES *Les Conklin*	5.00
___ SMART HANDICAPPING MADE EASY *William Bauman*	5.00
___ SUCCESS AT THE HARNESS RACES *Barry Meadow*	5.00

HUMOR

___ HOW TO FLATTEN YOUR TUSH *Coach Marge Reardon*	2.00
___ HOW TO MAKE LOVE TO YOURSELF *Ron Stevens & Joy Grdnic*	3.00
___ JOKE TELLER'S HANDBOOK *Bob Orben*	7.00
___ JOKES FOR ALL OCCASIONS *Al Schock*	5.00
___ 2,000 NEW LAUGHS FOR SPEAKERS *Bob Orben*	7.00
___ 2,400 JOKES TO BRIGHTEN YOUR SPEECHES *Robert Orben*	7.00
___ 2,500 JOKES TO START 'EM LAUGHING *Bob Orben*	7.00

HYPNOTISM

___ ADVANCED TECHNIQUES OF HYPNOSIS *Melvin Powers*	3.00
___ CHILDBIRTH WITH HYPNOSIS *William S. Kroger, M.D.*	5.00
___ HOW TO SOLVE YOUR SEX PROBLEMS WITH SELF-HYPNOSIS *Frank S. Caprio, M.D.*	5.00
___ HOW TO STOP SMOKING THRU SELF-HYPNOSIS *Leslie M. LeCron*	3.00
___ HOW YOU CAN BOWL BETTER USING SELF-HYPNOSIS *Jack Heise*	4.00
___ HOW YOU CAN PLAY BETTER GOLF USING SELF-HYPNOSIS *Jack Heise*	3.00
___ HYPNOSIS AND SELF-HYPNOSIS *Bernard Hollander, M.D.*	5.00
___ HYPNOTISM *(Originally published in 1893) Carl Sextus*	5.00
___ HYPNOTISM MADE EASY *Dr. Ralph Winn*	5.00
___ HYPNOTISM MADE PRACTICAL *Louis Orton*	5.00
___ HYPNOTISM REVEALED *Melvin Powers*	3.00
___ HYPNOTISM TODAY *Leslie LeCron and Jean Bordeaux, Ph.D.*	5.00
___ MODERN HYPNOSIS *Lesley Kuhn & Salvatore Russo, Ph.D.*	5.00
___ NEW CONCEPTS OF HYPNOSIS *Bernard C. Gindes, M.D.*	10.00
___ NEW SELF-HYPNOSIS *Paul Adams*	7.00
___ POST-HYPNOTIC INSTRUCTIONS—SUGGESTIONS FOR THERAPY *Arnold Furst*	5.00
___ PRACTICAL GUIDE TO SELF-HYPNOSIS *Melvin Powers*	3.00
___ PRACTICAL HYPNOTISM *Philip Magonet, M.D.*	3.00
___ SECRETS OF HYPNOTISM *S. J. Van Pelt, M.D.*	5.00
___ SELF-HYPNOSIS—A CONDITIONED-RESPONSE TECHNIQUE *Laurence Sparks*	7.00
___ SELF-HYPNOSIS—ITS THEORY, TECHNIQUE & APPLICATION *Melvin Powers*	3.00
___ THERAPY THROUGH HYPNOSIS *Edited by Raphael H. Rhodes*	5.00

JUDAICA

___ SERVICE OF THE HEART *Evelyn Garfiel, Ph.D.*	7.00
___ STORY OF ISRAEL IN COINS *Jean & Maurice Gould*	2.00
___ STORY OF ISRAEL IN STAMPS *Maxim & Gabriel Shamir*	1.00
___ TONGUE OF THE PROPHETS *Robert St. John*	7.00

JUST FOR WOMEN

___ COSMOPOLITAN'S GUIDE TO MARVELOUS MEN Foreword by *Helen Gurley Brown*	3.00
___ COSMOPOLITAN'S HANG-UP HANDBOOK Foreword by *Helen Gurley Brown*	4.00
___ COSMOPOLITAN'S LOVE BOOK—A GUIDE TO ECSTASY IN BED	7.00
___ COSMOPOLITAN'S NEW ETIQUETTE GUIDE Foreword by *Helen Gurley Brown*	4.00
___ I AM A COMPLEAT WOMAN *Doris Hagopian & Karen O'Connor Sweeney*	3.00
___ JUST FOR WOMEN—A GUIDE TO THE FEMALE BODY *Richard E. Sand, M.D.*	5.00
___ NEW APPROACHES TO SEX IN MARRIAGE *John E. Eichenlaub, M.D.*	3.00
___ SEXUALLY ADEQUATE FEMALE *Frank S. Caprio, M.D.*	3.00
___ SEXUALLY FULFILLED WOMAN *Dr. Rachel Copelan*	5.00

MARRIAGE, SEX & PARENTHOOD

___ ABILITY TO LOVE *Dr. Allan Fromme*	7.00
___ GUIDE TO SUCCESSFUL MARRIAGE *Drs. Albert Ellis & Robert Harper*	7.00
___ HOW TO RAISE AN EMOTIONALLY HEALTHY, HAPPY CHILD *Albert Ellis, Ph.D.*	7.00
___ PARENT SURVIVAL TRAINING *Marvin Silverman, Ed.D. & David Lustig, Ph.D.*	10.00
___ SEX WITHOUT GUILT *Albert Ellis, Ph.D.*	5.00
___ SEXUALLY ADEQUATE MALE *Frank S. Caprio, M.D.*	3.00
___ SEXUALLY FULFILLED MAN *Dr. Rachel Copelan*	5.00
___ STAYING IN LOVE *Dr. Norton F. Kristy*	7.00

MELVIN POWERS' MAIL ORDER LIBRARY

___ HOW TO GET RICH IN MAIL ORDER *Melvin Powers*	20.00
___ HOW TO WRITE A GOOD ADVERTISEMENT *Victor O. Schwab*	20.00
___ MAIL ORDER MADE EASY *J. Frank Brumbaugh*	20.00

METAPHYSICS & OCCULT

___ CONCENTRATION—A GUIDE TO MENTAL MASTERY *Mouni Sadhu*	7.00
___ EXTRA-TERRESTRIAL INTELLIGENCE—THE FIRST ENCOUNTER	6.00
___ FORTUNE TELLING WITH CARDS *P. Foli*	5.00
___ HOW TO INTERPRET DREAMS, OMENS & FORTUNE TELLING SIGNS *Gettings*	5.00
___ HOW TO UNDERSTAND YOUR DREAMS *Geoffrey A. Dudley*	5.00
___ IN DAYS OF GREAT PEACE *Mouni Sadhu*	3.00
___ MAGICIAN—HIS TRAINING AND WORK *W. E. Butler*	5.00
___ MEDITATION *Mouni Sadhu*	10.00
___ MODERN NUMEROLOGY *Morris C. Goodman*	5.00
___ NUMEROLOGY—ITS FACTS AND SECRETS *Ariel Yvon Taylor*	5.00
___ NUMEROLOGY MADE EASY *W. Mykian*	5.00
___ PALMISTRY MADE EASY *Fred Gettings*	5.00
___ PALMISTRY MADE PRACTICAL *Elizabeth Daniels Squire*	7.00
___ PALMISTRY SECRETS REVEALED *Henry Frith*	4.00
___ PROPHECY IN OUR TIME *Martin Ebon*	2.50
___ SUPERSTITION—ARE YOU SUPERSTITIOUS? *Eric Maple*	2.00
___ TAROT *Mouni Sadhu*	10.00
___ TAROT OF THE BOHEMIANS *Papus*	7.00
___ WAYS TO SELF-REALIZATION *Mouni Sadhu*	7.00
___ WITCHCRAFT, MAGIC & OCCULTISM—A FASCINATING HISTORY *W. B. Crow*	7.00
___ WITCHCRAFT—THE SIXTH SENSE *Justine Glass*	7.00

RECOVERY

___ KNIGHT IN RUSTY ARMOR *Robert Fisher*	5.00
___ KNIGHT IN RUSTY ARMOR *Robert Fisher (Hard cover edition)*	10.00

SELF-HELP & INSPIRATIONAL

___ CHARISMA—HOW TO GET "THAT SPECIAL MAGIC" *Marcia Grad*	7.00
___ DAILY POWER FOR JOYFUL LIVING *Dr. Donald Curtis*	7.00
___ DYNAMIC THINKING *Melvin Powers*	5.00
___ GREATEST POWER IN THE UNIVERSE *U. S. Andersen*	7.00
___ GROW RICH WHILE YOU SLEEP *Ben Sweetland*	7.00
___ GROW RICH WITH YOUR MILLION DOLLAR MIND *Brian Adams*	7.00
___ GROWTH THROUGH REASON *Albert Ellis, Ph.D.*	7.00
___ GUIDE TO PERSONAL HAPPINESS *Albert Ellis, Ph.D. & Irving Becker, Ed.D.*	7.00
___ HANDWRITING ANALYSIS MADE EASY *John Marley*	7.00
___ HANDWRITING TELLS *Nadya Olyanova*	7.00
___ HOW TO ATTRACT GOOD LUCK *A.H.Z. Carr*	7.00
___ HOW TO DEVELOP A WINNING PERSONALITY *Martin Panzer*	7.00
___ HOW TO DEVELOP AN EXCEPTIONAL MEMORY *Young & Gibson*	7.00
___ HOW TO LIVE WITH A NEUROTIC *Albert Ellis, Ph.D.*	7.00
___ HOW TO OVERCOME YOUR FEARS *M. P. Leahy, M.D.*	3.00
___ HOW TO SUCCEED *Brian Adams*	7.00
___ HUMAN PROBLEMS & HOW TO SOLVE THEM *Dr. Donald Curtis*	5.00
___ I CAN *Ben Sweetland*	7.00

___ I WILL *Ben Sweetland*		7.00
___ KNIGHT IN RUSTY ARMOR *Robert Fisher*		5.00
___ KNIGHT IN RUSTY ARMOR *Robert Fisher (Hard cover edition)*		10.00
___ LEFT-HANDED PEOPLE *Michael Barsley*		5.00
___ MAGIC IN YOUR MIND *U.S. Andersen*		10.00
___ MAGIC OF THINKING SUCCESS *Dr. David J. Schwartz*		7.00
___ MAGIC POWER OF YOUR MIND *Walter M. Germain*		7.00
___ MENTAL POWER THROUGH SLEEP SUGGESTION *Melvin Powers*		3.00
___ NEVER UNDERESTIMATE THE SELLING POWER OF A WOMAN *Dottie Walters*		7.00
___ NEW GUIDE TO RATIONAL LIVING *Albert Ellis, Ph.D. & R. Harper, Ph.D.*		7.00
___ PSYCHO-CYBERNETICS *Maxwell Maltz, M.D.*		7.00
___ PSYCHOLOGY OF HANDWRITING *Nadya Olyanova*		7.00
___ SALES CYBERNETICS *Brian Adams*		10.00
___ SCIENCE OF MIND IN DAILY LIVING *Dr. Donald Curtis*		7.00
___ SECRET OF SECRETS *U.S. Andersen*		7.00
___ SECRET POWER OF THE PYRAMIDS *U. S. Andersen*		7.00
___ SELF-THERAPY FOR THE STUTTERER *Malcolm Frazer*		3.00
___ SUCCESS-CYBERNETICS *U. S. Andersen*		7.00
___ 10 DAYS TO A GREAT NEW LIFE *William E. Edwards*		3.00
___ THINK AND GROW RICH *Napoleon Hill*		8.00
___ THREE MAGIC WORDS *U. S. Andersen*		7.00
___ TREASURY OF COMFORT *Edited by Rabbi Sidney Greenberg*		10.00
___ TREASURY OF THE ART OF LIVING *Sidney S. Greenberg*		7.00
___ WHAT YOUR HANDWRITING REVEALS *Albert E. Hughes*		4.00
___ YOUR SUBCONSCIOUS POWER *Charles M. Simmons*		7.00
___ YOUR THOUGHTS CAN CHANGE YOUR LIFE *Dr. Donald Curtis*		7.00

SPORTS

___ BICYCLING FOR FUN AND GOOD HEALTH *Kenneth E. Luther*		2.00
___ BILLIARDS—POCKET • CAROM • THREE CUSHION *Clive Cottingham, Jr.*		5.00
___ COMPLETE GUIDE TO FISHING *Vlad Evanoff*		2.00
___ HOW TO IMPROVE YOUR RACQUETBALL *Lubarsky, Kaufman & Scagnetti*		5.00
___ HOW TO WIN AT POCKET BILLIARDS *Edward D. Knuchell*		7.00
___ JOY OF WALKING *Jack Scagnetti*		3.00
___ LEARNING & TEACHING SOCCER SKILLS *Eric Worthington*		3.00
___ MOTORCYCLING FOR BEGINNERS *I.G. Edmonds*		3.00
___ RACQUETBALL FOR WOMEN *Toni Hudson, Jack Scagnetti & Vince Rondone*		3.00
___ RACQUETBALL MADE EASY *Steve Lubarsky, Rod Delson & Jack Scagnetti*		5.00
___ SECRET OF BOWLING STRIKES *Dawson Taylor*		5.00
___ SOCCER—THE GAME & HOW TO PLAY IT *Gary Rosenthal*		7.00
___ STARTING SOCCER *Edward F. Dolan, Jr.*		3.00

TENNIS LOVER'S LIBRARY

___ BEGINNER'S GUIDE TO WINNING TENNIS *Helen Hull Jacobs*		2.00
___ HOW TO BEAT BETTER TENNIS PLAYERS *Loring Fiske*		4.00
___ PSYCH YOURSELF TO BETTER TENNIS *Dr. Walter A. Luszki*		2.00
___ TENNIS FOR BEGINNERS *Dr. H. A. Murray*		2.00
___ TENNIS MADE EASY *Joel Brecheen*		5.00
___ WEEKEND TENNIS—HOW TO HAVE FUN & WIN AT THE SAME TIME *Bill Talbert*		3.00

WILSHIRE PET LIBRARY

___ DOG TRAINING MADE EASY & FUN *John W. Kellogg*		5.00
___ HOW TO BRING UP YOUR PET DOG *Kurt Unkelbach*		2.00
___ HOW TO RAISE & TRAIN YOUR PUPPY *Jeff Griffen*		5.00

The books listed above can be obtained from your book dealer or directly from Melvin Powers. When ordering, please remit $2.00 postage for the first book and 50¢ for each additional book.

Melvin Powers
12015 Sherman Road, No. Hollywood, California 91605

WILSHIRE HORSE LOVERS' LIBRARY

The books listed above can be obtained from your book dealer or directly from Melvin Powers. When ordering, please remit $2.00 postage for the first book and 50¢ for each additional book.

Melvin Powers
12015 Sherman Road, No. Hollywood, California 91605

HOW TO GET RICH IN MAIL ORDER
by Melvin Powers

1. How to Develop Your Mail Order Expertise 2. How to Find a Unique Product or Service to Sell 3. How to Make Money with Classified Ads 4. How to Make Money with Display Ads 5. The Unlimited Potential for Making Money with Direct Mail 6. How to Copycat Successful Mail Order Operations 7. How I Created A Best Seller Using the Copycat Technique 8. How to Start and Run a Profitable Mail Order, Special Interest Book or Record Business 9. I Enjoy Selling Books by Mail — Some of My Successful and Not-So-Successful Ads and Direct Mail Circulars 10. Five of My Most Successful Direct Mail Pieces That Sold and Are Still Selling Millions of Dollars Worth of Books 11. Melvin Powers' Mail Order Success Strategy — Follow It and You'll Become a Millionaire 12. How to Sell Your Products to Mail Order Companies, Retail Outlets, Jobbers, and Fund Raisers for Maximum Distribution and Profits 13. How to Get Free Display Ads and Publicity That Can Put You on the Road to Riches 14. How to Make Your Advertising Copy Sizzle to Make You Wealthy 15. Questions and Answers to Help You Get Started Making Money in Your Own Mail Order Business 16. A Personal Word from Melvin Powers 17. How to Get Started Making Money in Mail Order. 18. Selling Products on Television - An Exciting Challenge   8½"x11" — 352 Pages…$20.00

HOW TO SELF-PUBLISH YOUR BOOK AND HAVE THE FUN AND EXCITEMENT OF BEING A BEST-SELLING AUTHOR
by Melvin Powers

An expert's step-by-step guide to marketing your book successfully   176 Pages…$20.00

A NEW GUIDE TO RATIONAL LIVING
by Albert Ellis, Ph.D. & Robert A. Harper, Ph.D.

1. How Far Can You Go With Self-Analysis? 2. You Feel the Way You Think 3. Feeling Well by Thinking Straight 4. How You Create Your Feelings 5. Thinking Yourself Out of Emotional Disturbances 6. Recognizing and Attacking Neurotic Behavior 7. Overcoming the Influences of the Past 8. Does Reason Always Prove Reasonable? 9. Refusing to Feel Desperately Unhappy 10. Tackling Dire Needs for Approval 11. Eradicating Dire Fears of Failure 12. How to Stop Blaming and Start Living 13. How to Feel Undepressed though Frustrated 14. Controlling Your Own Destiny 15. Conquering Anxiety   256 Pages…$7.00

PSYCHO-CYBERNETICS
A New Technique for Using Your Subconscious Power
by Maxwell Maltz, M.D., F.I.C.S.

1. The Self Image: Your Key to a Better Life 2. Discovering the Success Mechanism Within You 3. Imagination—The First Key to Your Success Mechanism 4. Dehypnotize Yourself from False Beliefs 5. How to Utilize the Power of Rational Thinking 6. Relax and Let Your Success Mechanism Work for You 7. You Can Acquire the Habit of Happiness 8. Ingredients of the Success-Type Personality and How to Acquire Them 9. The Failure Mechanism: How to Make It Work For You Instead of Against You 10. How to Remove Emotional Scars, or How to Give Yourself an Emotional Face Lift 11. How to Unlock Your Real Personality 12. Do-It-Yourself Tranquilizers   288 Pages…$7.00

A PRACTICAL GUIDE TO SELF-HYPNOSIS
by Melvin Powers

1. What You Should Know About Self-Hypnosis 2. What About the Dangers of Hypnosis? 3. Is Hypnosis the Answer? 4. How Does Self-Hypnosis Work? 5. How to Arouse Yourself from the Self-Hypnotic State 6. How to Attain Self-Hypnosis 7. Deepening the Self-Hypnotic State 8. What You Should Know About Becoming an Excellent Subject 9. Techniques for Reaching the Somnambulistic State 10. A New Approach to Self-Hypnosis When All Else Fails 11. Psychological Aids and Their Function 12. The Nature of Hypnosis 13. Practical Applications of Self-Hypnosis   128 Pages…$3.00

The books listed above can be obtained from your book dealer or directly from Melvin Powers. When ordering, please remit $2.00 postage for the first book and 50¢ for each additional book.

Melvin Powers
12015 Sherman Road, No. Hollywood, California 91605